Also by Eithne Massey

THE SECRET OF KELLS

'This was one of the best books I have read …
I would give it 10 out of 10.'
Evening Echo (Reader Review)

'An exciting adaptation of the Cartoon Saloon's
Oscar-nominated film.' *Books Ireland*

FOR YOUNG CHILDREN

BEST-LOVED IRISH LEGENDS

'A book to keep and treasure.'
Irish Examiner

'A collection of old favourites including The Children of Lir
and The Salmon of Knowledge
in one handsomely illustrated volume for 4+.'
Irish Independent

THE DREAMING TREE

'A charming tale of a stranger learning to fit in.'
Books Ireland

EITHNE MASSEY is the author of *The Silver Stag of Bunratty* and *The Secret of Kells*, a novelisation of the Oscar-nominated animated film of the same name, and for younger children, *Best-loved Irish Legends* and *The Dreaming Tree*. Her work for adults includes: *Legendary Ireland: A Journey Through Celtic Places and Myths*.

WHERE THE STONES SING

EITHNE MASSEY

THE O'BRIEN PRESS
DUBLIN

First published 2011 by The O'Brien Press Ltd,
12 Terenure Road East, Rathgar,
Dublin 6, Ireland.
Tel: +353 1 4923333; Fax: +353 1 4922777
E-mail: books@obrien.ie. Website: www.obrien.ie

ISBN: 978-1-84717-277-8

British Library Cataloguing-in-Publication Data
A catalogue record for this title is available from the British Library

1 2 3 4 5 6 7 8
11 12 13 14 15

The O'Brien Press receives assistance from

Where the Stones Sing grew from the suggestion made by the Friends of Christ Church Cathedral, that a story, set in Christ Church, could be written for children and incorporate some of the history of the cathedral.

The Friends of Christ Church Cathedral, Dublin was formed in 1929 to assist the cathedral, making it one of the longest established groups of cathedral Friends in Britain and Ireland. Members of the Friends help support the cathedral's worship and conservation, its fine musical tradition and organise social events such as tours, lectures and other functions.

Back cover and internal photographs courtesy of Emma Byrne.
Front cover photograph courtesy of iStockphoto
Typesetting, editing, layout and design: The O'Brien Press Ltd
Printed and bound by CPI Group (UK) Ltd, Croydon, CR0 4YY
The paper used in this book is produced using pulp from managed forests

Contents

Dublin, August 1348 – Gull's Eye View

The white bird, blown up the Liffey by a sharp wind from the east, had a seagull's eye view of Dublin. Below him was a warren of narrow, crooked streets. Many of the timber houses were ramshackle, some of them on the edge of town little more than thatched clay cabins. To the west the river flowed past grey city walls past the yellow cornfields and green woods of the countryside; past the towers and abbeys and castles of its plain from the wild mountains in the west where it had first come out of the earth. Few Dubliners had ever been to those mountains. Dubliners loved to complain about their home town, bemoaning the crowds, the dirt, the crime, but they rarely left it.

The gull was a Dubliner, and was not going far. He perched on the roof of the great cathedral of Christ Church. The cathedral and the adjoining priory stood on a hill above the river and Fishamble Street wound around the edge of the priory lands. This was where the fish market was. The trestles were piled high with their silvery wares. At one end of the street was a pile of fish guts, stinking to heaven. The gull swooped and caught a mouthful, avoiding without effort the flapping hands of a fishmonger, who was loading up his wares for the evening. The gull flew west over the cloister of Christ Church to its main gate. There, he settled himself on the priory wall to eat his dinner in the light of the sinking sun. Below him were two ragged children, huddled against the wall. They were quarrelling.

The two children looked like brothers. They were both brown haired and had dark eyes, though the younger one's hair had more red in it and he was thinner and paler than the older boy.

'Let's go now. There is no one around, and I'm tired and cold and hungry,' the younger one was saying. But the other boy shook his head.

'No point going back to Ymna's if we have no food. There may not be anything to eat if we don't bring a couple of pennies with us. No, let's just try one or two more songs. There might be someone coming out of that inn, and drunk people are often generous.'

'But they stand around for ages and slobber and talk rubbish. And then demand songs from their youth that we don't know,' said the younger one. 'I couldn't believe it when that one with the greasy beard demanded *Sumer is icumin in*. It's nearly September.'

'Oh, Kai, we can make the words up. If they are far enough

gone they won't notice. We should really wait here until Pa comes back, anyway.'

Kai snorted. 'Edward, why are you always so *good?* Who knows when Pa is going to be back? It was dice he was playing, wasn't it, this time? With the farmers and shepherds who had come in with their sheep for the market?'

'Yes. I'm afraid so. Let's hope they don't look too closely at the dice. Come on, one last song. Then, if we get a penny or so, I promise you we will go buy a pie from one of the stalls before they close them down for the night.'

Kai sighed. 'Will we do "Fair Nell", then?'

The two began to sing, and, having finished his meal of fish guts, the seagull put his head to one side and listened. Not bad, he thought, not bad at all. The children had beautiful voices, high and sweet; though there were one or two moments when the voice of the older boy cracked and lost the note.

As they sang, three more boys came along the street. They were dressed identically in the black gowns and white cloaks that marked them as scholars in Holy Trinity Cathedral, known throughout Dublin as Christ Church. The tallest one, thin-faced and cold-eyed, stopped and glared at the singers. 'What have we here? Fairground children begging in the streets? And singing, disturbing the peace? Hasn't the mayor put out orders that those who do not work are not to be allowed within the city walls?'

The two children stopped singing and the younger one said, 'And what business is it of yours what we do?'

'My father says it is the business of every Dublin man, woman and child to make sure that the city laws are kept. And I won't have some beggar give me cheek. If you have any more to say I will stuff your words back down your crowing throat!'

The boy had no sooner finished then he found himself on his back in the mud of the street. Kai was on top of him, pulling his hair hard. Edward dived in an attempt to pull Kai off. But he soon found himself in a fight with the two other boys, who had not hesitated to join in the scrap. Quite a few blows had been exchanged – Kai was particularly pleased with the one that had gone squarely into the thin boy's nose – when the fight was stopped by a stern voice.

'Children! What's going on? Roland, Jack, I am ashamed of you! And Tom too! You are a disgrace to the priory, fighting in the streets like hobbledehoys!'

Two more people had come along the street. The one who had spoken was dressed in a white gown with a black cloak over it and a cross hung around his neck. The voice and the words were angry, but Kai, looking up at him from the ground, thought that this little monk's face looked good natured. As if he were more used to smiling than frowning. The monk was old and quite plump and his hair – what little there was of it – was white. His back was rather stooped, and he had dark eyebrows over very bright blue eyes.

The three boys stood up and said nothing, simply looked embarrassed as the thin boy tried to mop up the blood from his nose with his sleeve. He was handed a handkerchief by the monk's companion. She was a tall lady, dressed in sombre colours but in very fine cloth, and wearing a cloak trimmed with sable. She had pale gold hair and a sad, calm face.

Now she spoke:

'We heard singing as we came along the street. Please, will you sing for us again?'

Edward looked meaningfully at Kai. Surely this fine lady would be good for a penny or two at least? They began their song again. To their surprise, the three attackers joined in with the singing, and music filled the street.

When the song was over, the children looked expectantly at the couple. It seemed that the lady was as generous as they had hoped, for she drew her purse out from under her dark violet cloak. But instead of throwing the money into the shawl at their feet, the lady, a shilling in her hand, handed it carefully to Edward.

'That was beautiful, boys,' she said. 'You both have very fine voices – though yours, I think, is beginning to break. What are your names?'

'We are of the name Breakwater, and it please you, madam.' It was the younger who spoke. 'I am Kai and this is Edward.'

The lady smiled.

'And I am Dame Maria de Vincua, and this is my friend, Brother Albert, Canon of the Priory of Christ Church, which is the great building behind this wall. And are you from Dublin? I don't think I have ever seen you here before.'

This time it was the older boy who answered.

'We do not live here, though we have been in Dublin before now. We have come from the south, with our father. He is a musician, a medical man, and an astrologer. He can pull teeth and cure aches and make love potions and predict the future of any child, any baby born.'

Both children had been trained from an early age to advertise their father's wares to passing strangers. But now Edward was sorry he had said anything, for the lady's face changed. She suddenly looked even sadder than before.

Brother Albert interrupted hastily, 'That is most interesting, but it is your voices that concern us rather than your father's business. We have been discussing a most pressing need ...'

'Heigh-ho, what's the to-do here? What mischief has my flesh and blood been up to?'

A dark-haired man came strolling down the street, smiling. Ned Breakwater was exceptionally tall, a feature he sometimes regretted, for it made him more noticeable then he might otherwise have wished to be. But in any company he would have been noticed, for he was a handsome man with a glint in his eye and a laugh that rang out very loud and very often.

'What's this? What need is it that my children and not I can fill? 'Tis a strange thought, for, you must believe me, I am a man of many parts. I am an apothecary, a teller of fortunes, a seller of cures and futures. I am a man who can turn my hand to any task I might be set, if it needs a ready wit to do it. I am at your service; Ned Breakwater is my name, though for some reason ...' his smile grew wider, 'I am sometimes called Ned Longshanks.'

He took off his cap and bowed low to the lady, so low that his dark head almost touched the ground.

The canon looked unimpressed and the lady merely lifted one golden eyebrow, as if she was not quite sure if she believed all that Ned Breakwater was saying.

Then Brother Albert said courteously, 'Thank you for your offer, but I fear we do not need any of those services you mention. It is your children's voices we need, or at least the voice of one of them. This lady here, Dame Maria de Vincua, is as well known for her piety as she is for her wealth in this town of Dublin.'

The lady placed a restraining hand on Brother Albert's arm. 'Brother, pray do not ...'

'No, do not interrupt me, Maria, it is nothing but the truth.'

He smiled and continued, 'Dame Maria has lately suffered a most dreadful tragedy, for her son died these two months gone. Young Philip was a great lover of music, and a most promising singer. For that reason, and for the love of God, the lady has decided to perform an act of great charity. She has made a generous donation to the priory. One of the things she most especially wants is for four choirboys to sing every day in the Chapel of St Mary the White, in the cathedral. She will pay for the boys keep and their education as long as they do so. We already have three boys in the choir; these young rascals here. But we have been desperate to find a fourth boy, a boy with a voice like your son's. Would you like to have your child educated and fed, and perhaps have the chance to become a monk himself?'

Ned looked thoughtful.

'He would live in the priory and be looked after there? I do not know. But perhaps it might serve – what think you, Edward?' He was looking at the older boy.

But now the woman interrupted, 'Pray you sir, a moment. I think it is the younger child we should wish to have. Your elder son's voice is wonderful, but it is beginning to break. In any case, the younger child is more of an age with the other choirboys. His name is Kai, is it not? A strange name. I have not heard it before.'

There was a silence for a moment. The two children looked at their father with wide eyes. Ned coughed.

'He is called after the foster brother and seneschal of that most famous and noble king, the legendary King Arthur of Britain. My wife's people are descended from that great knight, the family is partly Welsh, you know. So it is my little Kai you would wish to have serve at the cathedral. God's teeth, I do not know. What say you, Kai?'

The younger child glared fiercely at Ned Breakwater.

'No, Pa, no.'

The three boys from the priory had been looking on in surprise. Two of them, thought Kai, looked nice. One had black shining hair and very black eyes, and stood waiting with his head on one side and a faint smile on his face. He reminded Kai of a blackbird; he had the same curious, bright eyes. The other was taller and more solidly built, with fair hair cut in a fringe and wide blue eyes. When they saw that Kai was looking at them they both grinned. It was clear that they harboured no hard feelings about the fight. But the boy who had started the battle, the thin-faced boy the canon had addressed as Roland, looked furious. Now he interrupted angrily, 'Don't tell me you want to bring that brat into the priory? To share our lessons and our table? He stinks!'

Brother Albert said sharply, 'Roland, hold your tongue. I have often had cause to speak to you about the evil that comes from your mouth. This boy has the voice of an angel. And one does not judge any child of God by the clothes they wear or the money they have in their pockets. Tell me, boy,' he turned to Kai again, 'can you read? And do you know any Latin?'

'Indeed he does,' Ned Breakwater answered. 'My children are both scholars. I have taught them well, despite our travelling life.'

The children grimaced. They wondered what their father would say if he was asked about their teacher, Gilbert. He certainly would not mention that Gilbert had been an ex-monk. Gilbert had left his monastery in disgrace after dipping into the altar wine one too many times. But he had not left empty handed; he had taken some of the monastery's treasures with him. After he had used up all his ill-gotten gains, he had made a new career for himself from selling fake holy relics. The Breakwater family had teamed up with Gilbert on the road to Wexford and he had travelled with them. He had taught the children Latin in exchange for a share in their food.

Now the lady said, 'And what of the child's mother? We should speak to her. Will she not have something to say?'

Ned sighed. 'That fair lady is dead these many long years,' he said. 'But I think – can you excuse me awhile? – I must take my son away for a few moments to discuss this idea with him. We will not be long.'

The lady smiled. 'We have time. We will wait here until you come back with your decision. But I would not willingly take a child from his father if he does not wish to go,' continued the lady. 'That would not serve God in any good way.'

She placed her hand gently on Kai's shoulder. 'Child, you

must come to the cathedral of your own free will, or not at all. But I think you will find that the monks are kind and you will be warm and fed through all the coming winter months.'

She cast a glance at the thin, ragged clothes that Kai was wearing, but said no more.

Kai, dragged unceremoniously away by Ned, whispered fiercely, 'Pa, I cannot do it, you know that I cannot.'

'I know nothing of the kind. This is a most wonderful opportunity to get into the priory. Stay there a couple of months and you'll hear a whistle at your window in the night. Then you can let your dear old pa in. I'm sure the holy canons have good pickings in their treasure house ... chests upon chests of gold and silver!'

As always, it was impossible to tell if Ned Breakwater was joking or serious. He was a trickster, not a thief, but Kai never really knew what he might decide to do next. But this must be the most dangerous trick he had ever tried to play. And Kai did not want to be part of it.

'No, Father, no. They would be bound to find out.'

'Now there is no need for you to shake your head at me like that. They will not find out, not if you are careful. As careful as I know you can be. They are all so innocent, these canons, they will suspect nothing. And you will be safe and sheltered there. It won't be for long, in any case. Then I will send you a message and we can be off on a boat to Wales before the canons have woken from their godly slumbers.'

There was another fierce shake of the head from Kai.

'There is no way it can work. We are sure to be caught. And anyway I'm not going to let you in to steal their things, the fat monk was nice. And the lady was lovely.'

Ned Breakwater shrugged.

'Then it's off out onto the road again tomorrow, for I have not a penny left and I think I dare not play dice in this town again. How will that be with you?'

Kai's face dropped. To be on the road again with no money in their pockets was a horrible thought. A sharp wind blew up from the Liffey and Kai remembered that winter was on the way. Last winter had been very bad, with weeks of snow and ice. The priory would indeed be warm and dry. And the choir boys had looked well fed and happy – well, all of them except Roland. But Roland, the boy who had started the fight, seemed to be somebody who rarely looked happy, no matter how kind people were to him. Kai made a decision.

'Very well then. I'll go with them. But Pa, I'm not going to let you in to rob their treasure. And if they find out my secret, you must come and get me, right away. Do you promise me that?'

'If they do find out your secret, I promise you I will come to you, though the demons of Hell bar the way. I give my word to you, child. Nothing will stop me. Send a message through Ymna, her people will be able to find me. Now, let's go back and tell them what we have decided.'

Roland looked dismayed when they returned and broke the news that Kai was to go to the priory. Edward too had a worried look on his face. But the canon and Dame Maria were delighted. Dame Maria said, 'Come back with me to my house. I live not far from here, though outside the gates. It's down by the river near the hospital of St John the Baptist. We will clean you up and find you some warm clothes, something to wear under the priory tunic and cloak. Then you will be fit to make your introductions to the prior.

'Brother Albert, will you go ahead and make a place ready for the child? And you Kai, I will leave you for a moment to say your farewells to your father and brother, and you can catch up with me. Just go westwards through the New Gate and along St Thomas's Street.'

No sooner had she left them than Edward turned to Ned and said fiercely, 'What in Beelzebub's name have you done now? What plot are you brewing? Can you not imagine what trouble there will be if they find out?'

Ned shrugged his shoulders and laughed. 'But they won't, for my little kitten is a wonderful actor, are you not, Kai?'

The children looked at each other. Their father was always like this: teasing, laughing, making everything a joke. Always asking his children if they did not want to have an adventure. Most days, Edward and Kai answered with a decisive *No*. An adventure was very often the last thing they wanted to have, especially if it involved being cold and hungry. 'Having an adventure' sometimes meant midnight flights from farm-houses and inns, and hiding in barns during the day so they would not be caught by the angry men their father had tricked. At other times it involved getting stuck half way through windows or explaining to disgruntled ladies that their father's magic potions did not always work. What both children wanted more than anything else was to live like other people, in a house, with four solid walls. To see the same thing day after day. To be bored, rather than cold and hungry and frightened, rather than constantly having to live on their wits.

And yet they both loved their father. Everyone loved their father. He was funny and loving and clever, and would do anything for them: spending his last pennies on a toy or a sweetmeat for them, and doing his best to make sure that they were kept safe in the rough life they lived. Now Kai took Edward's hand.

'Brother, listen, it will be only for a short time. And you know that things have been very hard, lately. If you want to stay in Dublin, whatever the monks give me to eat, I'll keep part of it, and will meet you here to share it.'

Edward shook his head. 'No, if you are safe in the priory, I have my own ideas about what I want to do. Now I will be able to follow my own road. I – I have been offered work, father, an apprenticeship with Giles the stonemason, here in

Dublin. Do you remember the last time we were here; I went down to his yard? This time I went down again, and tried my hand at working a piece of stone. And he says I have a real gift, and he would be happy to teach me. There is always work for a mason, he says. But I did not say anything, because I could not leave the two of you alone. But now Kai will be in Dublin, so I will stay too.'

It was not often Ned Breakwater looked taken aback, but now even he looked as if he thought things might be moving too fast for him.

'Good Lord, a child of mine a respectable craftsman, and another in the bosom of the church – who would have thought it? Though your mother's people were masons, so perhaps it is the blood from that side of the family that has come out …'

'I thought you said to the lady that our mother was descended from Lord Kai of the court of King Arthur,' said Kai.

Ned Breakwater grinned. So did Kai.

'Tch, him too, of course. We all have a great many ancestors. Hard to keep track, really. And as they say, "When Adam delved and Eve span, who was then a gentleman?" Or some such words … Well, it seems that you have made up your mind and there is little I can do about it. And I am glad you are here to keep an eye on Kai, Edward. Now Kai, get you gone as fast as you can after Dame Maria, in case she should change her mind. And have a good look around her house for me while you are there.'

'I told you I wasn't going to open any locks for you,' was the response, and then Kai took off at a run towards the New Gate.

Edward looked at Ned Breakwater. Even though he knew that his father loved to live on the edge of danger, he could not believe that he had agreed to this masquerade.

'Pa, Pa,' he said, 'of all the mad things you have ever done, this is the maddest. Have you any idea of the trouble we will all be in if the canons find out that their new choirboy is a girl?'

His father did not reply, but the gull, making his way back towards the river, gave a mocking cry into the east wind. The sun was beginning to sink in the west. Down below him, Dubliners prepared for night. From above, the city was a toy, neatly boxed in by the sea to the east and the mountains to the south. East was where strangers from the sea had come, century after century; and in the mountains to the south the wild Irish lived. Dubliners said that they ate their young. To the north, the great river formed another boundary. Dominating all were the castle and the cathedral. Guards patrolled the battlements of the castle, and the towers dotted along the city walls. As he flew by Wood Quay, the gull swept down to take a closer look at something. Among the ships docked there, he noticed a family of rats run deftly along a rope that tied one of the boats to the moorings. They were black rats, and the gull decided against trying to catch one. Rats were savage creatures, best left alone.

Dame Maria

Kai made her way westwards, hurrying through the narrow streets as best she could while avoiding the waste from the city horses, dogs and pigs that littered her path. She was nervous as to what might be in store for her in Dame Maria's house. A bath meant taking her clothes off. It might also mean the end of this masquerade before it had even begun.

Meanwhile, Brother Albert led the three boys up the hill and through the western gate of the priory. They were silent now as the little monk continued to scold them.

'Really boys, I don't know what Dame Maria must be thinking. I am only glad you were not seen by anyone else, brawling in the streets. It would have brought such disgrace to the priory. Now, go and clean yourselves up as much as you can before supper. I want you down in the refectory as soon as possible. We can't have you keeping the brothers waiting. Hurry now. I don't know what can be done about that nose, Roland, it's turning an impressive shade of

purple. Perhaps you had better come with me to the infirmary straight away, and we will see what we can do to bring down the swelling.'

Tom and Jack went to the wash house to clean themselves up as best they could with cold water and soap. In between flipping their washcloths at each other, they talked about the new addition to the choir.

'So what do you think of the new boy?' asked Tom.

Jack shrugged. 'Hard to tell yet, but I think I like him. I like the way he took on Roland, didn't put up with any of his old rubbish, and he's a good fighter.'

'I think there is something just a bit odd about him,' said Tom. 'But I can't say what it is, exactly. He can certainly sing. And he does seem nice enough. And anyone who doesn't like Roland is fine with me.'

Tom couldn't stand Roland. Nor could Jack. They had joined in the fight with him on the principle that he was one of their own, and anyway why pass up a good scrap, but not out of any loyalty to him as a friend. He was not an easy person to get along with. Apart from anything else, he was a snob, and never missed an opportunity to let the two other boys know that he thought himself much better than they were.

Jack was an orphan. He had lived in the monastery almost all his life. He had been found as a baby, left at the gate of the city one night and discovered by the watchman. No one knew where he came from, and the watchman, a man named Martin, had sold him to one of his friends, a woman who had used him when she went begging. People always gave more generously to a mother with a child. But the rest of the time she had neglected him, and Brother Albert had come upon him, dirty and crying, dressed in rags, sent out to beg alone when he was no more than three years old. The monks had taken the little boy in then, and looked after him ever since. Jack had only vague memories of the time before he lived in the priory. He loved the canons, the only family he had ever known, especially kind Brother Albert. But sometimes the quiet, ordered life drove him mad. He had grown into a boy full of life and mischief; full of the devil, as Brother Malcolm, one of the crankiest of the monks, put it sourly. He spent much of his time trying to escape the priory, hanging around the stables in the city, for he loved horses. If he was not there, he could be found wandering down to the river to where the ships were docked. Sometimes he would wander eastwards, going out as far as the sea. There he would spend hours chatting to the sailors and fishermen who plied their trades around the sloblands of the bay.

Tom, on the other hand, had only arrived at the monastery at the beginning of the summer. News had come to Brother Albert of the miller's child who sang like an angel in the Hospitallers' church in Kilmainham, the village to the west of the city. He had gone to hear him sing and had asked

Tom's parents if they would agree to send him into the priory as a choirboy. Tom's parents had been so proud of the honour to their child that Tom had not had the heart to tell them that he would have much preferred to stay at home. No one in the Oquoyne family had ever been brought to the great cathedral, or received an education beyond knowing how to weigh wheat and flour and count money. But Tom had loved his life with his noisy, cheerful family and he certainly didn't want to be a monk. He particularly missed his little sister, Edith, who was only a year younger than he was. He just wanted to stay in Kilmainham and learn the miller's trade like his father. But in the end, although he found life in the priory strange, it had not been as lonely as he had feared. Brother Albert was very kind and Jack was great fun. No one could complain about a quiet life with Jack around, showing his new friend the various ways to sneak out of the priory and explore what was going on in the city of Dublin.

Jack had been delighted to have someone he described as 'normal' come to the priory. Before that the only person of his own age in the priory had been Roland. When Roland had arrived in the priory just after Easter, he would hardly talk to Jack at all. And then, when he did start to talk, he drove Jack mad. He never stopped boasting about his father, who was somebody very important in the City Assembly. Roland was never clear about exactly what he did and the boys hadn't even seen him yet. According to Roland he was over in England, bringing important messages to the king. Neither Jack nor Tom could wait for him to come back and take his son away.

Now their conversation was interrupted by the arrival of Brother Malcolm. He took hold of Jack's ears and pulled him towards him, glaring into his face.

'Come along, quickly now, you are late already. Really, Brother Albert is far too soft on ye. And what's this I hear about you dragging poor Roland into trouble?'

Tom was so outraged by the unfairness of this, he could only stand with his mouth open. Jack, who had had years of experience when it came to Brother Malcolm, laughed. Brother Malcolm always defended Roland, because his father was rich and powerful, and like Roland, Brother Malcolm was a snob.

Jack said, 'I don't know what Roland has been telling you, but you it's pure rubbish, Brother. Roland is well able to get into fights all by himself.'

'Gross impudence and lying! We will see what the prior has to say about this!'

They made their way to the refectory, the great dining hall where everybody ate together, but luckily, Brother Albert had already spoken to the prior about their evening's adventures. When Brother Malcolm began his complaint, Prior Robert merely raised his hand for silence and signed to the Kitchener, Brother Reynalph, to begin the prayer the monks said before meals.

In most priories the choirboys ate separately, but in Christ Church there were only fifteen monks and it made less work and more sense for everyone to eat together. Also, Dame Maria had made it very clear that she wanted the children to be treated well. This meant that they ate what the canons did, not just the leftovers, as was the case in some priories. As the diet of the priory was quite bland and boring, Roland complained about the food constantly, and even Tom had to agree that it was nothing to get excited about: bread and weak ale, various types of soup, large quantities of salted fish or eels, peas and beans and onions and on feast days the treat of chicken or goose or some other fowl. Sometimes meat and sweet things could be seen being carried into the prior's private rooms, but that was only when there were important visitors from the castle or from the archbishop's palace coming to see him. Usually the prior dined at the top table in the refectory and ate what everyone else ate.

This evening, the meal was interrupted by the arrival of Brother Albert with the new choirboy. Kai was now looking much cleaner, though very tired. It had been a long day.

She had enjoyed her trip to Dame Maria's house. She didn't at all mind becoming a little grubby in pursuit of a good time, but she hated not being able to get clean again and her rags were filthy. After she had given a final hug to her father and Edward, she raced after Dame Maria. She had caught up with her very quickly. As she reached her, she gave a final look back at the walls of the priory and the cathedral. Dame Maria's eyes followed her look and she smiled.

'Isn't the cathedral wonderful?' she said. 'I love the way it stands on the hill over the river, looking as if it is on guard, watching the water and the hills in case danger comes to Dublin. It is our refuge, much more so even than the city walls or the castle. It will be wonderful for you to live there. And interesting. The prior is an important man in the city. Apart from the Archbishop, he is probably the most respected religious person in Dublin.'

'And what about St Patrick's?' Kai had spent the earlier part of the day sitting against the wall of Dublin's other cathedral. It lay down in the hollow on the southern side of the city walls, facing out towards the hills.

'St Patrick's is a godly, goodly church, but it is not as old or venerable as Holy Trinity; and it does not have its wonderful relics. You will see them soon. Or have you been inside the cathedral already?'

Kai shook her head. She had only sung outside the walls of the cathedral, never inside.

'It's a beautiful place. The High Altar is a work of such beauty! And there is the Talking Cross, and the Staff of Jesus, passed down by St Patrick, both great relics. Hundreds of pilgrims come to see them. The canons have chests of other relics stored in the crypt. And the relics of great St Laurence himself are held there. Have you heard of him? He was the cathedral's greatest archbishop.'

But Kai was more interested in the Talking Cross.

'Does the cross really talk?'

Dame Maria nodded.

'It has not done so for many years, but it has been said to cry out when a man told lies in front of it. You look doubtful. Do you not believe in miracles, child?'

Kai was not sure what to reply. She had seen Gilbert take a broken shoe and call it St Sylvester's sandal, some old stones and call them the Tablets of Moses. She had seen her father perform many tricks in the marketplace, so that people would believe that these shoes and stones could cure illnesses. People had called them miracles. So she had her doubts about anything that was supposed to be magic or a miracle. Yet at the same time she had seen strange things that could not be explained. Some people, like Ymna, the washerwoman they stayed with when they visited the city, seemed to have special powers. She always seemed to know they were coming to visit her before they arrived. She stood silently, but luckily, Dame Maria was diverted by meeting an old friend and the subject was forgotten when they started on their journey again.

They went through the gate of the city, Dame Maria nodding and smiling at the guards as if she knew them well. Outside the walls the fair green was full of the noise and smell of the sheep that were brought to market at the end of the summer. While they made their way through the sea of bleating, woolly faces and down past the abbeys of St Thomas and the hospital of St John the Baptist, Dame Maria chatted to her, explaining that her house had belonged to her husband. He had been a merchant who had died when their son had been just a baby.

'It's a fine house, and I love the fact that it is so near the river and is a little bit away from the noise and dirt of the city.'

Beyond St James Gate there were no more rows of houses. It was almost like the countryside; here there were fields and scattered houses, and views through fruit and nut trees down to the river. Kai fell in love with Dame Maria's house as soon as she saw it. It was a tall stone house with a neatly thatched roof. There was a grey wall around it, but this was broken by an archway. Dame Maria led Kai under the archway and in through the front door, which opened into a hall. The walls were a sparkling white and the high ceiling and west-facing windows made it seem full of light. Everything was clean, everything was orderly. At one end was a large fireplace with a fire burning brightly in it. Along the mantelpiece was a row of polished pewter and bright pottery plates. The room was simply furnished with a long table and benches and two large chairs by the fireplace, a cabinet gaily carved and painted with birds and flowers and one or two chests placed under the windows. The wood shone, the pewter glinted in the firelight and the place smelled of fresh lavender and rosemary. A door led to the kitchen quarters, equally bright and orderly, and a stairway led upwards to the chambers. These too were bright, the beds and chests hung with finely sewn tapestries. Kai could not resist going over to examine one, which showed a stag hunt in a forest. Dame Maria came and stood behind her, touching the tapestry with one gentle finger.

'I made that for Philip when I was waiting for his birth. He loved it very much, and used to ask me to make up stories about it.'

She sighed and then went to one of the chests, where she began to pull out some clothes.

'These are Philip's. He was a little taller than you but you will grow into them soon enough. The monks will give you a surplice to wear for when you are singing in the church, but these will do for other times. No doubt they will give you a cloak as well, but here, take this in case you need extra warmth.' She picked up a cloak. 'See, this is where Philip tore it, trying to climb up one of the walls in the city. He was a wild child.'

'How did Philip die?' The question was out of Kai's mouth before she realised what she had asked. There was silence in the room and Kai felt dreadful. She wanted to know about the boy whose death had made such a change in her life, but now Dame Maria looked so sad that she felt really bad for her. She wanted to go over to Dame Maria, to hug her, try to make her feel better, but she couldn't do that. It would not be something a boy would do and it might give away her secret.

Dame Maria smiled sadly and went to the northern window of the room.

'Come and see. You see the garden and the gate that leads down to the river?'

Kai looked out and saw a garden filled with late summer colour. The apples and pears were beginning to ripen into gold and russet among the green leaves of the trees. There were beds of bright flowers and scented herbs and a stone wall with a gate in it. She could see over the wall to where the river wound its way towards the sea. There was a small rowing boat moored at its edge.

'He was playing, of course, messing about on the water in his boat. But the boat overturned and he was trapped beneath it. He should not have been out alone. I always told him he should not go out on the water by himself. But that day I was not there to watch. By Jesu, I will never forgive myself for that …'

'And you have no other children?'

'No, Philip was an only child. He was all I needed. There are those who told me I should have married again to give him a father and to have other children. But no one could replace my Geoffrey. Or my Philip, now. Oh Kai, if you could have seen him. Or heard his voice; his voice was like gold. I have not even a picture to remember how he looked. It is only sometimes, when I hear the choir sing, that I think that I can hear him too ... which of course is just my mind playing tricks. But, now, enough of that. What about you, child? Have you been travelling with your father ever since you were born?'

'As far back as I can remember. My mother died when I was very little so I don't remember her at all.

Kai was surprised to find that her voice sounded shaky. She was so used to not having a mother that she rarely thought about it. But to have a mother like Dame Maria must have been lovely ... She fingered the piece of pink coral on the silver chain, the only thing she had to remember her own mother by. She kept it well hidden under her clothes. It was her most precious possession. Her father had told her that mother had worn it all the time. He had also told her that coral had special powers, and could protect her from disease and harm.

She saw Dame Maria watching her and moved her hand away from her coral. She had to pull herself together. She couldn't allow herself to cry like a girl.

'We have travelled all over the place. Not just in Ireland but across to England and even once to France. My father cannot stay still.'

'You have been to France! You must tell me all about it. You have travelled far more than I ever have. The furthest I have been outside Dublin is Tallaght. Or was it that pilgrimage I went on to Swords? But it must be hard to be out, travelling the roads all the time. And have you no other family, no grandparents or aunts or uncles who might look after you so you would not have to live so rough a life?'

Kai shook her head. 'No, there is just the three of us. I think my father quarrelled with his family, but he never speaks about it. It's not so bad really; every day is different. Exciting.'

Even to her own ears, her voice sounded doubtful. Dame Maria said briskly, 'There's nothing too exciting about singing for alms in the shadow of a cold wall with the night coming on. However, I see you are a loyal child, which is all to the good. Do you want to keep your own clothes? You must get into these things here and I'll bundle the rest up for us to carry up to the priory. Listen, the bells of Christ Church are ringing – we must not be late. But first, go down to the kitchen and get yourself clean. I told Damaris to leave out soap and hot water in front of the fire. We must hurry back.'

Kai felt herself shaking slightly. She hoped against hope that she would be left alone while she washed and changed. However, she was pleased to hear that her voice was quite steady when she asked:

'Can we have a look at the garden before we go back?'

'Yes, if we don't delay too long. Do you like gardens?'

Kai nodded. There was something so nice about the idea of having one's own garden, of planting things and actually being there long enough to see them come up out of the soil. Dame Maria led her down to the kitchen and, to Kai's great relief, left her alone. To make sure she wouldn't be interrupted, Kai dragged two heavy stools in front of the door and washed and changed as quickly as she could. Then she joined Dame Maria where she was gathering herbs outside. This garden is full of music, thought Kai. There was the sound of the water beyond the wall, and birdsong and the warm buzzing of bees. Dame Maria showed her the vegetable plot, with its last crops of beans and peas and the marrows and the onions. Then they visited the pear and apple trees that already had tiny fruits hiding in the leaves, the fruit bushes and the herb garden where Dame Maria grew healing plants for the medicines she made. They gathered some honey from the hives that were lined against the western wall, and Dame Maria told her that she could take one of the combs back to the priory for the monks.

On the way back into the house, she showed Kai the still-room with its long table and shelves with vials and retorts, and herbs hanging everywhere. Here Dame Maria dried and distilled roses and lavender and many other plants. She used the mixes to make everything from polish to potions for those who were sick. The room smelled wonderful.

Kai looked around her, thinking how lovely it would be to spend time in Dame Maria's house, helping in the garden and the kitchen and the stillroom, and learning how to make beautiful things like the tapestry upstairs. But she could say nothing about this – no boy would ask to learn how to sew tapestries! She wondered how she was going to cope with being a boy all the time. Although she had always acted as a boy while out on the streets singing, up to now she had been able to relax and be as girlish as she liked when she was alone with her father and her brother. Now she couldn't do that. Now she would have to watch herself every minute of every day. She would have to fight her corner and shout with the best of them. And her fellow choirboys *were* probably going to fight with her, if today's adventure was anything to go by. Although she had a strange feeling that during their last scuffle, Jack had got in a kick at Roland, rather than actually doing her or Edward very much harm.

The Priory of Holy Trinity

By the time they got back to Christ Church Kai was very tired. Dame Maria left her at the gate of the priory and she was led by the gate-keeper to the refectory, where Brother Albert introduced her to the brothers. All the brothers had different work within the priory – some of them looking after the kitchens and the cellar, some riding out to collect the rents from the priory's farms in Dublin and beyond, some keeping the accounts. There were too many of the brothers for her to take in all their names at once, but one or two faces stayed in her head: Brother Stephen because he was so tall and thin and pale and had such a gentle smile, and Brother Malcolm because he was very handsome and seemed to be looking down his nose at her. The prior, Robert, was a tall, stout man, with a high colour and a hooked nose. He looked energetic and efficient, but he smiled at her kindly.

'Welcome, Kai Breakwater. I hope you will be happy here

and learn to praise God well with the holy gift that the Lord has given you. And I see that you have come bearing a gift of sweetness from our benefactress, Dame Maria. Her honey is the best in Dublin. You have done good work today, Brother Albert. Dame Maria has made a generous bequest and it will fill my heart with joy to hear singing in the Chapel of the White Mary of Dublin every day.'

'Kai's voice is wonderful. He could become the best singer in our little choir.' Brother Albert said eagerly, and while Kai felt rather odd to have herself discussed as if she was not there, she could not help but be pleased. Now the prior raised his eyebrows and asked, 'Is his voice as sweet as Roland's?'

'Sweeter, I think. As sweet as the honey he has brought us from Dame Maria.'

Jack poked Tom and whispered, 'And let's hope his nature is sweeter than Roland's too.'

Unfortunately, the prior overheard him.

'Jack, I beg of you, control yourself. We will not have insults made to our brothers in the Lord.' But even the prior could not resist a smile, as if he knew that Jack's comment about Roland's lack of sweetness was a fair one.

Kai was soon to discover how very sour Roland could be. He had hated the very idea that Kai, a beggar child, was being allowed into the priory. The fact that this new choir member was competition for his place as the soloist of the choir only made him angrier. He frowned when, after the meal had been finished, Brother Albert told the boys to take Kai to their dormitory. 'We are going to sing in the church, but you children do not have to attend this particular office.'

Brother Albert saw Kai looking puzzled, and continued:

'The services are called offices. We pray and sing at regular stages during the day and night. You and the other boys are here to sing the special afternoon service in memory of Philip. You will do that every day, but you will also attend some of the other services and sing with us. And of course you will sing with us on Sunday at High Mass. But you look weary, child. It has been a long day for you. Go along now; it's time you were all in bed.'

The children's rooms were near the Great Gate, beside the guest chambers and the prior's quarters. The monks slept in a dormitory over the chapter house and kitchen, to the east of the cloister. Jack chattered non-stop as they made their way through the cloister, the central square garden which the priory buildings were built around.

'We'll show you the rest of the priory tomorrow, the chapter house and the scriptorium and the kitchens. And the piggery and the stables. And Hell, of course.'

'Hell?' said Kai.

'Pay him no heed,' said Tom. 'It's just the name of the little dark passageway that leads from the priory to Fishamble Street.'

'Is it called Hell because it's so dark?'

Jack crossed his eyes ferociously.

'That and because there is a demon lives there. The Dolocher. He appears in the shape of a giant black boar with bristles and HUGE tusks.'

Tom said, 'Oh give over, Jack. He is just trying to frighten you, Kai. Jack loves telling his stories, but don't pay any heed to them … And here we are.'

The children entered a long white room, almost as narrow as a passageway. Along one wall there were windows looking out over the cloister. For a horrible moment Kai thought that they all had to sleep together in the same room. Then she realised that one side of the room was divided into separate cells, each with a tiny arched window above the bed. Each boy had a separate little cell. The partitions were made of lime-washed white wood, which meant that the children could still talk to each other when they were in bed. Kai was soon to learn that Jack loved to keep everyone awake and shivering with stories of witches and goblins, of fairy creatures like the puca and the banshee, of ghosts and other creatures of the night. But now they all went into Kai's cubicle.

Roland, who had come along with them with a sulky look on his face, pulled at the cloak Dame Maria had given Kai and spoke for the first time, 'You must have stolen this from somewhere – it's far too good for you. I am going to confiscate it.'

Kai felt a rush of fear. At the best of times she hated to be pulled at, and now, so tired that she was close to tears, the last thing she wanted was another tussle, a tussle in which her companions might discover that she was not a boy after all. She pulled the cloak closer around her.

'Leave it be! she said. 'Dame Maria gave it to me!'

'Leave it be!' Roland mimicked her in a high-pitched voice. 'Oh, aren't we the high and mighty one, with our friends like Dame Maria! But I don't believe she gave it to you! You stole it like the thieving brat you are!'

They were now both pulling at the cloak, and Kai was shaking, terrified that it would tear, or worse, that her secret might come out.

But Jack pulled Roland back and said, 'No, Kai is telling the truth. I know that cloak – it belonged to Philip. Look, there's the tear he made that time we had the fight with the choirboys from St Patrick's and we had to escape over the archbishop's wall.'

'Did you know Philip?' Kai asked.

Jack nodded. 'He was one of my best friends. It was horrible when he died. Old Jenny Greenteeth got him in the end.'

'Jenny Greenteeth?'

'The witch that lives in the water. She pulls people to their death when they go on the Liffey.' Jack's voice had changed to deep sepulchral tones. 'You can always tell that she's around, lying in wait, when you see the green duckweed that grows where she is sleeping. Tom knows all about her.' Jack shivered dramatically and Tom nodded.

'She's a dreadful creature. All the millers tell stories of her. I have never seen her but my father's uncle has, and he says he was never so frightened in his life.'

Kai was not sure she believed in Jenny Greenteeth, but when she saw that Roland had gone very pale she realised that he did.

Now Tom put his hand on Roland's arm.

'That enough, Roland,' he said. 'Leave the cloak alone. You are just making trouble and you know you are in Brother Albert's bad books already for teasing Quincunx.'

'Who's Quincunx?' asked Kai.

'The kitchen cat. The terror of the kitchen mice. Do you like cats and dogs?'

Kai, who had been chased by large numbers of farm dogs, guard dogs and even the occasional hunting dog, considered for a moment.

'I am sure I like cats,' she said. 'I'm not sure about dogs.'

Roland cut in, 'Scared of them, are you? You're worse than a girl!'

'I'm not scared of them,' said Kai, wondering if she would need to mention this small lie in confession. 'I just don't especially like them.'

'You will have to come and visit our mill out at Kilmainham,' said Tom. 'We have a little farm there too. We have loads of puppies at the moment and I know you will like *them*. We have kittens as well. We nearly always have kittens in one or other of the barns.'

Kai was puzzled. 'If you have a home of your own, why are you here?' she asked.

'It's a great honour to be brought to sing in the cathedral,' said Tom, in a resigned voice. 'And anyway the mill is going to be left to my older brother, so they have to find something to do with me. I might become a monk, though I'm not sure I'd like it. Jack here is an orphan, so it's almost certain you will become one of the monks, isn't it?'

Jack shrugged. 'I don't think I would make a very good monk. It's so quiet here! What I would really like to do is become a sailor or a fisherman and spend my life out on the sea. Or maybe work with horses. I love horses. I'd ride any horse, even the puca. Last April I went out with the seneschal when he rode out to collect the rents from the farm at Glasnevin – it was the best day! And I love singing too, of course. I really can't really decide which is my favourite thing of all.'

Kai decided she would make an effort with Roland, who had finally let go of her cloak but was still standing in the cubicle swinging from foot to foot with a sour look on his face. She had a feeling he was always the one left out in this group. She had so often been the one left out that she hated seeing it being done to anyone else.

'Is singing your favourite thing?' she asked him. Roland sneered at her.

'No it's not. I don't even like it, even though I *am* the best singer in Dublin. But then I am the best at *anything* I do. It's a pity nobody here realises that. I have been stuck here in this place because my father has had to go away on the king's business. I shouldn't be mixing with rabble like you at all. And as soon as my father gets back to Dublin he will take me away from here. He's going to be given a really important job, perhaps even be put in charge of the king's government in Ireland. Then you can be sure I will have nothing to do with you – except perhaps ask my father to put every one of you in the pillory!'

'Let's hope he *is* made Justiciar,' Jack said. 'Then maybe you will go off and live in the castle and not be around to boast and cheat and sneak any more.'

'And that would indeed make us *all* very happy,' said Tom.

Kai resisted the temptation to nod in agreement. So much for making an effort, she thought. There really didn't seem to be much point with Roland.

It was strange to sleep in her little bed, knowing that her father and her brother were not close by. Indeed, she had no idea where her father was, though she thought it likely he was in Ymna's. Ymna, though long settled in Dublin, was related to the fairground people, the wanderers like the Breakwaters who lived on their wits and called nowhere home. Kai lay awake for a long time, wondering if at last she *could* call somewhere home. But for how long? How long was this new deception going to work? She had a feeling that Roland already suspected something; she had noticed him watching her, staring at her during dinner. It was going be hard enough to live a lie without someone spying on her all the time. She tried to think of how she needed to be careful. For certain, tomorrow she had to be awake before the boys, to be up and dressed and washed. She just hoped she would be able to wake up in time. She would listen for the bells giving the number of the hours. She tossed restlessly. It was lonely, in the dark, with nobody she could talk to for comfort. But then there was a low *Brrrr* and something soft and warm landed on her chest. Opening her eyes, she could just make out a white furry face and a pair of glowing green eyes.

'You must be Quincunx,' she whispered.

The reply was a deep purr. The cat settled on her chest and curled into sleep, and the comforting feel of the warm fur and the gentle noise of the purring soon sent Kai to sleep too.

Rat's Eye View

Dark. Dark was good. Dark was safe. The darker the better. Noise and clatter and shouting – not so good. Humans and that bloody cat that had been the family's torment throughout the voyage. But now the ship had stopped. Though still rocking, the boat no longer moved forward into the waves. Time to explore. Hmm … Shapes, barrels, good, and something that smelled REALLY good. The rat crept down the rope, and slithered noiselessly onto the stones of the quay. It lifted its head, sniffing the air. That way – that was where the smell of humans and human food was strongest. It crept up the hill towards the cathedral, stopping only to scratch itself vigorously. It had been a long voyage and it felt as if it were being eaten alive by fleas.

The next day began with the bells calling everyone in the priory to prayer. Life in the priory was strictly ordered, with the services in the church at the centre of all the activity. Even during the night the monks rose to go to the chancel

to pray. Although the children did not have to go to the night-time service, they did have to get up before dawn so they could sing lauds in the cathedral.

Kai went along, although she could not yet join in the singing. The choir entered the cathedral as the sun rose, streaming through the great eastern window and lighting the gold and jewels on the high altar, making it the focal point of brightness. At its very centre was the great cross, the cross that had spoken and was now at the heart of the devotions of almost everyone who came to pray in the cathedral. But as she walked through the nave, Kai was not looking at the altar but up at the roof of the cathedral. It rose into an arch above her, making her feel as if she was looking for the sky through the branches of a forest. The pillars of the arches were beautifully carved. Stone flowers grew out of them; dragons curled around them; angels sang from their tops.

Tearing her eyes away from the wild extravagance of the carvings, Kai looked down at the floor. Here there were more wonders, for the tiles made intricate, colourful patterns under her feet. She saw lions and eagles and even a group of little foxes walking on their hind legs, dressed as pilgrims and following each other around in a circle. Kai could hardly keep her eyes on where she was going, as the children made their way up near the high altar, to the part of the cathedral called the choir.

As Kai kneeled and listened to the monks' voices rising

upwards in harmony, she peered through the fingers covering her eyes in prayer. She could see the tombs that lined the walls: jolly-looking, chubby bishops with their feet resting on little dogs; solemn knights with their swords by their sides; ladies with elaborate headdresses and their hands folded piously. One little tomb looked as if it belonged to a child. It was dark and shadowy in the cathedral, but the darkness was not frightening, because it left space for the light to come through the stained-glass windows. A bird's shadow flew across the glass, reminding Kai of the world outside. Dublin would just be waking up to face the new day.

Kai would learn to love these windows, telling herself the stories of the pictures they held: Noah's ark, with all the animals clambering on board; St Laurence, blessing the orphan children he had sheltered; the Queen of Heaven surrounded by stars; the Holy Ghost; the dove that was part of the Holy Trinity, after which the cathedral was named. She especially liked the Christmas windows. Here were the shepherds hearing the news from the singing angels; one of them had his hand over his mouth in shock. But the first time Kai gazed up at the windows, she noticed one that frightened her: a devil with a boar's head, dragging a very unhappy looking woman down into the fires of hell. She quickly averted her eyes to the carvings on the tops of the stone pillars. Just next to her was a carving of a flock of birds with children's heads nestling against the stone, their mouths open. She couldn't decide if they were singing or waiting to be fed. She thought proudly that soon perhaps her brother would be one of the masons that would carve new scenes in the stone.

The choir sang the first psalm and then there were a few moments of silent prayer. Kai thought how strange it was that people could never help coughing or sneezing or rustling during times like this. But finally there was total silence, and in that silence she thought she heard another sound: the faintest of whispers, the quietest of laughs. She looked around at her companions; nobody seemed to be paying any attention. She looked closely at the cross; perhaps it really could speak? But the sound had not come from that part of the cathedral. She shook her head. It had to be her imagination. So much had happened since yesterday, she was hearing things. Then her attention was brought back to the Mass. The choir, made up of the brothers and her three fellow-choristers, had begun to sing again. The sound was beautiful. As part of the choir even Roland seemed transformed into something better than himself.

After the lauds there was a light breakfast and then Brother Albert took Kai around to show her the different parts of the priory. As she had seen the night before, the priory was built around a central square, the cloister. It was covered in soft green grass, with a fountain in the middle. There were covered passageways lined with decorated stone arches on all four sides. The monks could walk around the square, reading or praying as they went. The cloister was enclosed by the cathedral itself to the north. To the east lay the chapter house and the kitchen, and the dark, half-underground alley known as Hell. The refectory was south of the cloister. To the west was the Great Gate, and Kai was given a quick glimpse of the prior's chambers with its coloured glass in the windows and its huge and elaborate fireplace. Brother Albert even brought her down to the crypt of the cathedral. It was dark and frightening, the very oldest part of the church.

'You have already seen some of our relics, the ones held in the cathedral, such as the great cross. And did you notice the relic of St Laurence, his heart held in the silver reliquary?'

Kai shook her head. She didn't like the idea of seeing anyone's heart, saint or not. Brother Albert continued, 'I will show you later. But this is where the rest of our relics are stored, along with the treasures of the cathedral.'

Kai thought of her father and tried not to listen. The less she knew about the cathedral treasures the better.

Finally, Brother Albert took Kai to the outbuildings of the priory. There were stables and bakehouses and brewhouses, and an infirmary which had a stillroom very much like Dame Maria's. Kai began to sniff the air, smelling something rather unpleasant, and Brother Albert, beaming, said, 'We are approaching the piggery. Because of the smell, it's a little outside the walls of the priory.'

Despite the faint smell, the piggery was cleaner than any piggery she had ever seen. Brother Albert introduced the inmates:

'That's Amby, short for Ambrose, and the darker one is Jerry – his full name is Jerome. The one beside him snuffling in the dirt is Ignatius, usually called Iggy. Iggy the Piggy. The two girls are inside the stye, they are called Augustina and Basilia.'

The little monk was gazing at the pigs with a proud expression on his face.

Kai coughed. 'Eh, do you mind me asking – where do the names come from?'

'Do you not recognise them? They are called after the Fathers of the Church. We'll be studying their works in class. The great thinkers of Christianity, my boy. These fine animals are named in their honour, although I did have to take the liberty of giving the sows female versions of Basil and Augustine.'

Kai wondered how she was going to feel when she came to the works of Basil, Ignatius and the rest of them in her lessons. It might be hard to take seriously the thoughts of someone who she would always see in her mind's eye as having a snout and a curly tail. But Brother Albert obviously had great respect for his pigs.

'We don't let them out at all, you know,' he said. 'It is a dangerous thing to allow pigs loose on the streets, for the pig as well as for humans. We feed them twice a day – that will be one of your jobs. Out in the streets, you never know what they might eat. The street pigs eat every kind of rubbish they came upon, and knock people over and cause mayhem with their squealing and stealing. So they are kept in here, though I sometimes feel they could do with a little more exercise.'

'Would you like me to take them out sometimes, for you?' Kai asked. She quite liked the idea of bringing one of these clean and intelligent-looking beasts for a walk. Brother Albert shuddered.

'A kind thought, but no, thank you. Jack took one of the piglets – it was Basilia, in fact – to bed with him once. He thought she was lonely, and of course she escaped and ran all over the priory and even got into the prior's bed. You should have seen the havoc she caused, rampaging around. And this was all going on in the middle of the night! Never again, never again. Ah look, there is Basilia herself coming out. She's a bit of a wild one. A touch of the Gaderene swine, perhaps. No, Basilia.' He poked the small black pig with his stick as she tried to bite Augustina. 'Stop it now, or you'll be seeing the inside of a frying pan sooner rather than later.' He turned to Kai, as the bells rang overhead. 'But now, time is moving on and we must get to class!'

Brother Albert, as well as teaching them singing, was to

educate them in grammar, arithmetic, Latin, and reading and writing. Kai found that the actual singing came easily to her, and her quick brain had little trouble learning the words of the psalms. Her first lesson in following musical notation was more difficult. But she loved the look of the notes marked on the huge pages of the psalter. The black shapes flew like birds among the words of the hymns, soaring upwards into the air, as the music had soared upwards into the stone of the cathedral.

Brother Albert was pleased with her progress, and when they broke for the midday meal he told her she could have the rest of the day free. He would stay with Tom that afternoon and try to get him to retain some of the Latin lesson in his head. Tom looked very doleful when he heard this.

As they ate, Jack suggested that they go down to the river and see if any new boats had come in, but Kai shook her head.

'Today I'm going to go to see my brother Edward. He's started an apprenticeship in the stonemason's yard over towards St Kevin's Gate. I'll go with you another day, though. I love going down to the river too.'

'Common children go down to the river to play in the mud,' said Roland. 'I have better things to do than go down *there.*'

'I didn't ask you to come, Roland,' said Jack, 'But Kai, if you are going past St Patrick's, be very careful. If any of the choirboys from there spot you going past wearing the priory colours, they will jump on you for a fight. We do the same to them if they dare come up the hill.'

He added, 'So Roland, so what *are* you going to do for the afternoon? Torture Quincunx? We all know it was you who tied that piece of metal to his tail.'

Kai, who had been known to rescue cockroaches from drowning, looked at Roland in horror.

'You can't possibly know it was me who did that,' said Roland.

Tom broke in:

'Yes we can. Because you are the only one here that would have done something that mean. It's your favourite thing, isn't it, watching animals in pain?'

But Roland only smirked as if he didn't care what anyone said about him.

'Well, then, prove it,' he said. 'You'll see, you can't. I'm far too clever to be caught.'

Kai left her companions and made her way across the Cornmarket and into the Liberties of St Sepulchre. Giles the stonemason had his yard there, where he worked on the carvings for the churches and monasteries of Dublin. Kai had met him the last time her family had been in the city. She had liked him, and his cheerful wife and his daughter Joan, who was just a little younger than her brother. Joan was brown haired and green eyed and very pretty and she had beautiful clothes that

Kai envied a little. She was always friendly and kind, though, and Kai had thought that, if she could have acted as a girl with Joan, they might have become good friends. She had a feeling that Edward also liked Joan a lot. Now he would be an apprentice living in Giles's house and would have a good chance to get to know her better. At least things were working out well for her brother, who, like her, had longed for a quieter life. Maybe they could both now live in a manner that did not involve trying to hang onto their father's cloak tails as he made his dizzy way through life. That was how her father made her feel, dizzy and excited but with the slight threat of a pain in her stomach. As if you had a hive of bees buzzing inside your head.

Even from outside the doorway in the wall that led to the stonemason's yard, Kai could hear loud hammering. She pushed the door open. Inside was a courtyard, full of noise and the fine pale dust from the stone that filled the yard. Half a dozen workers were banging away at blocks of stone with their chisels and mallets. She spotted Edward in one corner, but he did not see her. He was concentrating hard on the piece of stone he was working on. Even when she came right up to him, she had to shake his shoulder to get his attention. He looked up and smiled, then wiped his sleeve across his face, in an attempt to clear some of the dust that had gathered around his cheekbones. It smeared all over his face. It was not a warm day, but his face was covered in sweat.

Kai laughed at him. 'I see you haven't managed to get any cleaner since you left the road!'

'Katy!' Edward shouted the name in delight as he hugged her tightly. For her part, Kai almost jumped out of her skin. She pulled back from Edward. Too much hugging between brothers might make people wonder. 'Shhh,' she whispered. 'Remember.'

'Sorry, *Kai*, I mean. How are you? I like the fancy duds.'

A part of Kai wanted to tell Edward about how hard it was going to be to keep her secret from her new friends. Apart from anything else, her conscience felt grubby. She hated to deceive Tom and Jack and kind Brother Albert. And then there was the strange feeling she had had in the cathedral. Those voices – they had sounded so real. Had it been the cross, she wondered, speaking to her? But a cross would surely not laugh – and that had been a very distinct giggle she had heard. It gave her goosebumps to think about it. But she decided not to tell Edward, for what could he do to help? If she told him her worries, it would only make *him* worry too. And he seemed so happy now.

Kai grimaced as she answered, 'Dame Maria gave them to me. I feel so mean lying to her, especially as they belonged to her son. You should be wearing them! But so far everything is going well. Brother Albert is nice and I think I will make friends with two of the other boys who are part of the choir. I'm not sure about the third one. Well, to be honest, I am sure. He is a really horrible boy. And how are you?'

Edward's smile lit up his face. 'I'm so happy that this has all worked out so well. I love the work here and I'll be learning all the time. Master Giles says I'm good. He has already let me take on some of the simpler pieces – look, this is going to be in St Mary's, across the Liffey.'

Kai looked. Edward was carving a simple rosette into the stone. It would be one of dozens which would become part of the abundance of flowers and leaves, of small animals and angels which would decorate the abbey.

'This stone is quite easy to work in because it's soft, though you have to be really careful to treat it gently. Some of the other stone, like the granite Paul is shaping over there, is much harder and slower.'

They went over to where Paul was working. Paul was a tall young man with massive arms, but Kai could see that he was using all his strength with each stroke he made with his chisel and mallet on a large uneven rock. Beads of sweat stood out on his forehead and his jaws were clenched. He did not smile at either of them, just kept working at the stone.

'Hello, I'm Kai,' said Kai, holding out her hand to Paul. The young man just grunted and Edward pulled Kai over to where Master Giles himself was working a piece of golden-yellow stone.

'What's wrong with *him*?' asked Kai, looking back to where Paul continued to beat at the stone, a frown on his face.

Edward raised his eyebrows. 'I don't know. He has been nasty to me ever since I arrived. But come, have a look at this.'

Kai looked at the stone. It was the same type of stone that Edward had been carving and reminded Kai of the creamy stone of Christ Church.

'You must come back to see this piece finished – it will be wonderful. One day,' he told his sister, 'I will be allowed to put my own mark on the stone, so that in years and years in the future people will be able to look at some wonderful carving and know that it was me that made it, me, Edward Breakwater.

Kai grinned and couldn't resist a tease. 'Do you think they will care? And are you sure that the cathedrals will last so long?'

'Of course they will. They are made of stone. What could last longer than stone?'

Kai looked on as Master Giles, his forehead furrowed in concentration, worked with a tiny chisel and hammer on what seemed to be becoming a group of people. The noise of the chisel made its own music as Master Giles worked the stone. Looking more closely, she saw that the group was made up of musicians. Each instrument was delicately carved, each face was different. Edward spoke again. 'It's like magic, isn't it? The way he pulls the figures out of the block of stone. It's almost as if they are speaking to him, asking to be set free from the stone.' Edward's voice was low and reverent.

Kai looked at her brother in surprise. She had never heard him sound so passionate about anything.

Now Master Giles looked up from his work and smiled. 'Well, young Kai, greetings to you. I have heard that you have taken up residence in Dublin too. It will be good for your brother to have you nearby if your father goes off on his travels again. And I believe you are singing in the cathedral. That's a great honour indeed. We usually go to Mass in our own church, but we must be sure to all go up to hear you sing. Edward has a great voice too. I'm sure we are often going to ask him to sing for us in the evenings.'

Master Giles lifted his head as the bells of the city rang out. They had to stop their conversation until they had stopped. 'There now, it's getting late. I must keep working on this. It is for Christ Church itself. You two go into the house and Joan will get you some almond pastries and something to drink. But you must not wait too long to go back to the priory, Kai. The streets can be dangerous at night.'

As they made their way into the house, Edward said, 'He's a great master, isn't he? He treats me like one of the family. And he has said that he will look after my application to the guild, and even pay the fees, so that I can become a real mason. I can't ask for better than that.'

Kai nodded. She had heard stories of apprentices who were treated worse than slaves during the time when they learned their craft, and could do nothing about it. An apprentice had to stay until he was finished the long years he was bound to his master, or risk punishment. But Kai was sure that Edward would be more than happy here.

Now her brother asked her, 'Kai, has Father said anything about leaving?'

'I haven't seen him since we were both with him outside the priory yesterday. When he was muttering about getting me to let him into the cathedral. But I won't do it. I won't.'

'Oh, he was probably just teasing you. You know the way he loves to do that. Anyway, you might not have to worry about it for too long. I have heard news that Father was gambling with a group of sheep farmers and they are not happy with the way things turned out for them. Pa may find it is better for him to get as far as possible outside the walls of Dublin for a while. And then the archbishop has been preaching against beggars, and the mayor has been complaining about travelling entertainers. He says they do no work, just live off the labour of the good people of Dublin. Pa may find he has to get up and go. There's a part of me that would be almost happy if he did.

'Me too,' said Kai, guiltily. 'Even if he went for just a little while. It would be so nice to stay in one place and make some friends.'

That was one of the problems with having adventures and travelling all the time. She never got a chance to get to know other children. Everywhere she went, she was the last one in, an outsider coming to a place where people already had best friends. And just when she got to know somebody really well, Ned would arrive and break the news that it was time to move on.

That night Quincunx came to Kai's cell, mewing fretfully. He jumped on her bed and began kneading the bedclothes with his paws.

'Do you want to go out then, you brat?' asked Kai, and went to open the shutters in the tiny arched window over her bed. But when she looked out she jumped, for standing in the moonlight looking up at her was a cloaked figure.

Within a moment the figure had pulled down his hood. Kai saw it was her father.

'Pa!' she said. 'What is it? Where have you been?' She shivered. Surely her father was not trying to get her to sneak him into the priory already?

'I have been lying low, my dear. Those bloody sheep farmers are looking for me and are very persistent in their searching. It must come from looking for lost sheep … But I came to talk with you and Edward, before I go away for a while. How is it with you?'

'Good, Pa, better than it's ever been. Edward is very happy in Master Giles's house, and I am happy here too, in the priory. I want to stay here, for a while anyway.'

'That is what I have come to speak to you about. No, don't look at me like that – I have not come to ask you to let me into the priory. Not this time. Now, listen to what I have to say. I fear it may not be safe for you to stay here. In fact, I have changed my mind – I have decided that you should leave Dublin and come with me.'

'Leave Dublin? Why?' Kai was astonished.

Her father looked grim.

'I have heard stories about a terrible disease. It has already killed hundreds of people in Europe. It's said that it has made its way as far as the English ports. And if the infection has reached that far, it is bound to come to Dublin as well. Dublin is a city and a port; boats come in from England every day. The disease is a dreadful one. It is almost always mortal. I cannot bear to think of you or Edward catching it. So, I am leaving the city, going up into the mountains with some of the fairground people. I want you and Edward to come with me. You will be safer out of Dublin. But we must get on the road tonight. Will you come with me now?'

Kai couldn't believe that her father was doing this to her. Again. Just as soon as she had adapted herself to whatever mad plan Ned Breakwater dreamed up, he changed it. This had happened so many times. And she had done as he wished. But not this time. This time she was going to do what *she* wanted. And she did not want to go back out on the road again. Not with winter coming on. Not with the possibility of new friends like Jack and Tom and Dame Maria and a safe, ordered life in the priory.

She shook her head. 'No, I told you, I'm happy here in Dublin. And Edward is the same.'

'Aye, I have already been to talk to him. He too has refused to come with me. But you, Kai, you are younger. I beg you to come to where you will be safe from the plague. I would wait a while, but, as you know, I am in some difficulties with those sheep farmers. And with some guardsmen. And with some ladies of the city. I fear I cannot stay to watch out for you any longer.'

Her father sounded as if he were close to tears, but Kai knew what a good actor he was – nearly as good as herself. She suddenly felt very angry.

'When did you ever watch out for me? Go away, Father, and leave me here in peace. You must go now, straight away. I can hear someone moving.'

It was true, she could hear someone shifting in the cell to her right – the one where Roland slept. She couldn't bear the thought of him finding her talking to her father, so she said again, her voice sharp, 'Father, you have to go. I have nothing else to say to you.'

She saw her father's face change, and realised with a sense of shame that she had really hurt his feelings.

He compressed his lips.

'Very well, child. If that is what you want. But if you need help, be sure to leave a message with Ymna. She will be able to find me. I wish I did not feel that I was leaving you in danger. But perhaps the plague will not reach across the sea, and you will be safe with the good brothers. Go with God, my child. I will not be so far away that I cannot come to help you.'

Her father turned and moved into the shadows, and Kai, with a sudden pang, wondered when she would see him again.

The Disappearing Cat

Kai soon became used to the routine of life in the priory. No word of any sickness came to the brothers, and she breathed a sigh of relief that she had not taken to the road with her father. She had seen Ymna the washerwoman once, delivering her washing to the prior's room, but had dodged behind a pillar so as not to be spotted by her. The Breakwaters had known Ymna for years. She lived with her children and her father in a small house with a large laundry attached. She never stopped working, and the muscles on her arms were huge from constantly beating linen clean and wringing it out to dry. She had always been very kind to Kai, but she also had a mouth to match her muscles. She talked all the time, never thinking before the words came out of her mouth. Kai was afraid that if they met she would blurt out something that would give away Kai's secret. It was bad enough trying to keep that secret herself.

There were times when it was really hard to keep the

fact that she was a girl hidden. Each morning, the children rose to sing lauds with the monks, sleepy eyed and chilled from having left their warm beds for the cold stone of the church. And every single day, Kai had to be sure to be up and washed and dressed before anyone else. Luckily, Quincunx had decided he wanted to sleep in her cubicle and woke her up in the morning before the first bell rang. She became very fond of the furry white cat. He was very affectionate but also seemed to have his own secret life, disappearing off for long periods. Everyone in the priory was used to him turning up out of nowhere after he had not been seen for hours.

But then Quincunx went missing. The cat was seen one evening beside the fire in the kitchen and had disappeared the next morning. That was not so unusual, but when there was still no sign of him the morning after, Kai began to worry. When Roland appeared in a hood trimmed with white fur, Jack had his theories about what had really happened to Quincunx, but no one wanted to believe him. Everyone knew that Jack's imagination was a little overactive.

But Roland had made some remarks about how close Kai was to the cat, and she was afraid that he might really have done something to hurt him. Roland hated all animals, but cats especially. 'Everyone knows that cats are close to the devil. Witches keep them, as familiars,' he said. They were discussing Quincunx's disappearance in the schoolroom.

The conversation had started when Kai told Brother

Albert about how worried she was that something had happened to the cat.

Brother Albert replied, 'Roland, there is no other animal closer to the devil than we humans when we chose to do evil. It would be well for you to remember that. Now, as regards souls, Augustine, for example, says that animals do not possess them. But not everyone agrees with him. And then, we can't really know, can we? The Lord's creation is a mystery which we know very little about at all ... And whether animals have souls or not, it is our duty to look after them and treat every living thing kindly.'

Roland replied, 'My father says that animals are here to serve us; that's what God put them on Earth for. It doesn't matter how we treat them. We are their masters.'

Kai couldn't help butting in angrily: 'It matters how you treat anything alive! It matters if something feels pain!'

Roland's face was set in a stubborn expression. He was not about to change his mind. 'Not if they don't have a soul. Animals don't go to heaven, only humans do. We are God's children and animals are not.'

Brother Albert interrupted. 'That's enough, now, boys. It's time for a story. But I want you all to keep a good eye out for Quincunx. Whether he has a soul or not, I want to be sure that he has not come to any harm.'

Brother Albert took their education seriously, and they worked very hard. But every day, towards the end of the morning, he would tell them stories, sometimes religious ones but also folktales and fables. Although she often got bored with arithmetic and grammar, Kai loved these kinds of lessons almost as much as she loved the singing. And Brother Albert was delighted that she worked so hard; she had become his best pupil. Tom tended to go into a daydream; Jack was too restless to listen properly and Roland didn't think anyone could tell him anything he didn't already know.

During these times, Brother Albert talked to them about magical places: Prester John's kingdom far to the east of the world, the disappearing island of Hy Brasil off the west coast of Ireland, the Elysian Fields where the heroes of old lived in eternal sunlight. One day, as he was telling them about the Garden of Paradise and the choirs of angels singing there, Jack interrupted him, as he so often did.

'I think I'd rather be out in the fields of Elysium than in a garden. Or in a boat sailing to Hy Brasil.'

'Paradise is not a small garden, you know,' said Brother Albert rather shortly. He didn't take interruptions to his storytelling well. Kai, watching him, felt that when Brother Albert talked of these magical places he was imagining himself really there, far away from the worries of life in the priory. Sometimes he didn't want to come back. But now he smiled.

'And you know that the church is a boat too, bringing us all to salvation,' he continued. 'That is why the part of the church where the congregation stands is called the nave. Can anyone tell me what Latin word this comes from?'

None of them could, and he sighed.

'Not even Kai?' He looked at her, but Kai, although she thought she might know the answer, said nothing. She had already answered five questions this morning. She didn't want to seem too much of a teacher's pet.

'It comes from *Navis,* of course, meaning ship. Because when you look up, you could be looking into the bottom of a ship. And because, as I said, it carries us all safe to the Lord. Really children, I don't know if anything goes into your heads at all.'

'But the Elysian fields, Brother. Do they have horses there?' persisted Jack.

'Ah, the Elysian Fields. A pagan notion, but one which shows how close the virtuous pagans could come to the idea of Paradise. They were the fields where heroes went after death, so called from the Greek word meaning "reeds", for reeds grew in them. It was a place of eternal happiness, where good people walked and talked together and were at peace. And no doubt, Jack, in your Elysian fields there would be horses. In mine, there would be a library and a great deal of singing. And Kai, what would you have in yours?'

Kai thought hard. 'A house. A nice square stone house and a garden. A garden with flowers and birds. And of course everyone I love.'

There was a derisive snort from Roland, seated behind her.

'You talk like a girl!' he sneered. 'And I suppose you will be sitting there in heaven, wearing a dress, doing embroidery in your pretty garden! With a sweet little pussy cat at your feet!'

'That's enough, Roland,' said Brother Albert sharply. 'What about you, Tom?'

Tom had to be poked hard by Kai. He had been asleep. He didn't know what the question was and Brother Albert sighed and moved on.

'And what about you, Roland? What would be in your Elysian Fields?'

Roland snorted. 'I don't believe in such rubbish. It certainly wouldn't be up to much if any of you were there with me!'

Brother Albert sighed again.

'Uncalled for and unpleasant, Roland. I fear you have become like the child in the story, unable to open your mouth without toads jumping out. I would like you to write for me, in Latin, a description of what you see in your paradisal landscape. We will discuss it at class tomorrow.'

Roland scowled at Kai. She whispered to Jack, 'Look at him, he's blaming me for getting him into trouble. As if he wasn't able to be totally obnoxious without any help at all from anyone else.'

The bell for the midday meal rang out. Jack jumped from his seat, nearly knocking the bench over.

Brother Albert sighed again. 'And Jack, try not to make quite so much noise as you leave the room. I don't know how many times I have had to tell you to go quietly.'

After their meal, it was time for them to go to sing in the cathedral, in the side chapel of the White Mary of Dublin. The chapel held a small oak statue of the Virgin Mary, and every day fresh flowers were placed in front of it. This was where Dame Maria had asked to have her son remembered. Today Dame Maria herself was already there, praying, and Jack whispered to Kai, 'She's always there when we arrive. Sometimes Tom and I have thought we have seen her lips moving, as if she's speaking to someone.'

'Maybe she's just praying?' suggested Kai.

Tom shook his head. 'No, she has her head on one side, as if she is listening for something – or someone – as well as talking.'

Brother Albert frowned at the children to be quiet, but Kai watched Dame Maria, and it was true that she did sometimes look as if she were listening to something or someone. By the end of the service she looked much more at peace than at the beginning, as if she had somehow been comforted. She usually stayed and talked to the children and Brother Albert. She always remembered to bring some sweetmeats or fruit from her garden for them. After this, the children were free until supper, and after supper there was the final office of the day which the children sang with the monks.

Kai soon made good friends with Jack and Tom. Jack was the more adventurous of the two; if there was trouble to get into, he was always in the thick of it. Tom was quieter but he was always up for any adventure Jack might lead them into. Together, they explored the docks, where the great ships moored in the sludge of the Liffey. Kai thought their high masts and flying sails some of the most beautiful things she had ever seen. The children would spend hours watching the strange-looking people and the fascinating cargoes they carried: bales of rich silks, exotic wines and fruits, spices and perfumes, and lovely yellow stone from England for the continuing work on the two cathedrals and the castle.

Jack was especially excited the day a shipload of thoroughbred horses was unloaded. They went wild coming off the boat, kicking and snorting and trying their best to run away. Jack ran down from his perch on the dock and offered to hold some for the groom, who was cursing soundly as a flying hoof narrowly missed his head.

'You'm just be making them worse, I'd say,' he said in a thick Bristol accent. 'But if you'm can hold onto any, and help me get them to the stables in Cook Street, I'll give thee a farthing.'

At this, Kai slid down the bank and went to help Jack. A farthing was not to be sniffed at. Tom sat for a moment. He was more nervous around horses than he would ever admit to Jack and Kai. In fact, he hated being near them. He had been kicked by one of the mill horses when he was very small, and he had never forgotten the pain and the shock, and the sight of the horse's red, rolling eyes. He still had nightmares about it. Even now sometimes, after he had been running or jumping, the scar on his knee throbbed and he was reminded yet again of that horrible moment. But he did not want to be left behind. He drew a breath and followed them down.

Kai was used to horses, and did her best to help, and Tom overcame his fear enough to lead one or two of the quieter horses along. But Jack was the star. It seemed he had only to lay his hand on the beasts and whisper in their ears for them to calm down immediately. It was as if he had some special link with the beasts that made them quiet as soon as he touched them. They worked out a system where Jack first soothed each animal and then one of the other children led the beasts to where the groom was ready to drive them to the stables. When the horses were unloaded, they went along with the groom, with Jack circling round the beasts, rather like a sheepdog, thought Kai. Though, unlike a sheepdog, he did not yap or nip, just laid his hands on the horses that looked restive and spoke calmly and encouragingly to them.

'Where did you learn to do that?' Kai asked him.

He shrugged. 'Nowhere. It just comes to me. Maybe my

father was a horse thief!'

'Or a knight,' said Kai.

Jack snorted. 'Say that to Roland and see how he reacts!'

'This fine herd is going to market on Michealmas, later in the month,' said the groom. 'They should fetch good prices.'

Jack was looking longingly at an especially beautiful foal, pure black with a white splash on his forehead. Kai caught his eye and he grinned ruefully. Neither of them would ever have the money to buy such a fine beast.

When they got to the stables, the groom pulled out his purse and doled out a halfpenny to be shared by Kai and a by now rather pale Tom. To Jack, he gave a penny – a whole day's pay!

'You saved me a muckle of time and trouble, lad,' he said. 'And if you should ever want to work with horses, you come see me and I'll have a job for you. You have a gift with them that not many have. Not even myself.'

Jack smiled and tossed the penny in the air.

Dinny

But as the autumn drew on, the children had less time to explore. There were days after the service when Brother Albert would ask one or other of the children to help him in his works of charity around the city, tending the sick and the poor. The canons of the cathedral, unlike many monks, had the right to leave the monastery, and many of them, like Albert, felt it their duty to help where they could. Other monks, such as the ones at Thomas Court and St John the Baptist to the west of the city, brought those who were ill into their monasteries and looked after them there, but the canons of Christ Church went out into the homes of Dublin, bringing food and medicines and warm clothes. Kai did not mind going out with Brother Albert. He was always so cheerful, even when he had to face the most desperate cases. But even he grew worried as the number of illnesses in the city grew greater and began to show some disturbing symptoms.

Kai also really enjoyed visiting Dame Maria, who asked

her to help with gathering the autumn apples and pears, and promised to bring her nutting through the hazel bushes along the Liffey when the time came.

One day, as they cut back the raspberry canes in her garden, she looked at Kai, puzzled. 'You are a very gentle little boy, Kai, but would you not rather be out with Jack and Tom, having adventures?'

Oh no, thought Kai. I hope she's not going to start suspecting something. But she smiled and said, 'I do spend lots of time with them too.'

This was true; she had had lots of adventures with her two friends. She smiled to herself as she remembered what they had been up to just the day before. The three of them had sneaked onto one of the boats docked in the Liffey and, thinking there was no one on board, they had gone into the captain's cabin. Jack had wanted to have a look at the mariner's equipment; he had been fascinated with the wooden astrolabe and the compass. But while Jack and Tom had been engrossed in examining the compass, Kai had heard a movement from the deck, and the three of them had had to dive under the bunk in the cabin and lie there, squashed tightly in, as a pair of leather sea boots appeared. Kai, who was on the outside, had the best view of what was happening. She deeply regretted this, when the whistling sea boots sat down on the bed. The sailor removed the boots and his hose, and then began to pare his toenails with a knife. She could feel

Jack's silent laughter at her back, barely contained, and the more he laughed the more she could feel it spreading to her. To make things worse, the dust under the bunk and the strong smell of feet made her want to sneeze. Luckily, the sailor was called outside just as he began to clean between his toes, and the children had managed to make their escape through the porthole and along the rope that kept the ship moored to land. They had arrived home to a scolding for being late and for the state of their clothes, but it had been worth it.

Any time she thought of their adventure she could feel the laughter rising again. But she knew she could not tell any adult about such escapades, especially not Dame Maria, who was such a gentle person. Kai liked these quiet times with her. There was something so restful about being with Dame Maria; she never hurried or shouted, and yet she seemed to get an enormous amount of things done. Like Brother Albert she was very busy helping the poor and sick in the city.

For now, Kai continued with her answer: 'And Tom is bringing us out to his house in Kilmainham next Saturday, for the day. It's his sister's Saint's Day and we are going out there for the celebrations.'

Dame Maria smiled. 'You will love it there. Here, let me send out some of my comfrey ointment with you. I know Alisoun, Tom's mother, will be happy to have some. With such a large family there is nearly always somebody tumbling or falling and bruising themselves.'

Saturday turned out to be a perfect autumn day, bright and cool. The children left the cathedral directly after lauds, having been given the whole day off from choir duty. It was less than an hour's walk to Kilmainham, but they wanted to be there as early as they could be so they could spend as much time as possible at the farm and the mill. Brother Albert had also asked them to gather some acorns in the woods for the priory pigs. He impressed upon them the need to be back at Christ Church before it got dark.

'For we live in lawless times, and you never know who might be out there on the road, lying in wait for travellers.'

Roland watched them go with a sulky face. Tom had invited him to come along, feeling it would be too mean not to ask him, but Roland had made it clear that he had no interest in visiting Tom's family. Now he seemed to be annoyed because he wasn't going with them.

'Should I ask him again? Tom said anxiously. 'Maybe I should, though I know he'll just ruin the day for all of us.'

Jack shook his head vigorously.

'Don't bother. He probably just wants the chance to say no and be rude to you, and make horrible comments about your family. We'll be far better off without him, won't we, Kai?

Kai had to agree. She had long since given up trying to include Roland in the fun they had together. 'I'm afraid so. Any time I have tried to be nice to Roland it has just made him nastier to me.'

They made their way through the early-morning streets. Although it was so early, there were signs of activity around. They passed where a market was being set up. As the traders emptied their big wicker baskets, piling meat and fish, autumn fruit and vegetables on the trestles that lined the street, they shouted greetings to the children. Already, pigs foraged underneath, hoping that something would fall down to their eagerly waiting snouts.

As the children went out past St James's Gate, which marked the boundary of the real countryside, on past Dame Maria's house, and further west, the scenery became a patchwork of fields and small stands of trees. Westward, there were the woods which grew wild and stretched for miles out beyond Kilmainham. Walking along, Tom explained that his father's mill was one of three on the Cammock, the little river that branched off the Liffey.

'One of them belongs to the Knights Hospitallers – you will see the walls of their priory soon. They are a very rich order who own almost all the land around Kilmainham. My father's mill has always belonged to his family though, and he supplies flour even to the Hospitallers. We have a farm too, and some orchards. And we keep a few horses. Though they are just farm horses, so I don't know if you will want to bother seeing them.'

'I will,' said Jack. 'Any horse is better than none.'

Tom could hardly contain his excitement as they came closer to the village of Kilmainham. He had not been home since the beginning of the summer. Part of him was very proud of his home, while another part was really sad because he realised that he could not go back to live there. He missed his family. He missed the noise and bustle and comings and goings of the mill.

Now he walked so fast that it was hard for Jack and Kai to keep up with him, chattering all the while.

'Can we stop for a moment?' said Jack breathlessly. 'I want to have a look at the horses in that field.'

Reluctantly, Tom stopped walking but could not stop himself from jigging up and down impatiently as Jack went over towards the horses. Kai smiled at him. Tom was usually the quietest of them all, the last one to react to anything. But of course he was going home; he had been born in the mill and lived there all his life. Unlike herself and Jack, he had a real home to go to. But at least, thought Kai, she had her father and her brother; poor Jack had no family. Yet it did not seem to bother him; he was smiling now, stroking the soft noses of the horses they had stopped to see. The whole herd had immediately raced over to him when he had called to them from the fence.

But Tom was urging them to move on. 'When we get to the top of the hill, we will be able to see the Knights Hospitallers' priory. Come, on. Look, there it is.'

The children saw a large group of stone buildings rising up beyond the walls that enclosed the priory. From where they were looking, it looked almost like a little village. Then they had reached the banks of the Cammock and Tom was racing the last bit of the journey. The mill house, old stone and golden thatch, stood before them, its door open as if to welcome them in. But as Tom led his friends into the kitchen and started to introduce his brothers and sisters to his companions, he realised one face was missing.

'Where's Edith?' he asked. 'Surely she's not lying abed on her Saint's Day?

'Poor Edith is not well at all,' said his mother, coming over to hug him and greet Kai and Jack. 'A summer cold, but she's shivering like a leaf, so she is staying in bed. She's very disappointed not to be able to get up to greet you, but you can go up to the chamber and see her if you wish.'

Edith, fair-haired and blue-eyed like Tom, was pale and, even under the mound of blankets and duck feather quilts, was shivering as if with cold. She hugged Tom tightly and smiled at his friends.

'I'm so annoyed that I can't get up,' she said. 'I was really looking forward to spending the day with you. But Tom, you go on and show your friends the mill and the farm, and come and see me later. Maybe I'll feel better then.'

Tom looked at his mother anxiously.

'It's just a summer cold, I'm sure,' Dame Alisoun said again, tucking the blankets more closely around her daughter. 'Or it could be the over-excitement of the day. Maybe the thought of too many sugar sticks! Now, you bring your friends around and show them everything. Perhaps Edith will be feeling better later and able to go out with you.'

So Tom began the tour of the farm. They went first to the orchard by the river and picked fruit to bring back to the canons. Tom led them from there to the oak wood along the riverbank where they gathered a sack of acorns for the priory pigs. There they stopped and paddled in the little river, splashing each other and laughing. But Jack was impatient to see the stables.

Taking a shortcut through the dairy, where the cows were milked, they reached the stables, where the great workhorses were kept. Tom shivered a little as he entered them: this was where the horse had kicked him when he was small. Kai looked at his pale face and asked him if he was feeling ill.

'I'm fine,' he said. 'But I'm dying to show you the mill.'

It took a while to get Jack away from the horses, but when they eventually went to the mill the giant mill wheels fascinated him almost as much. Tom's father was there. After greeting them kindly, he left them alone, and went to deal with a customer who had come to collect flour.

'Tom will be able to tell you as much as I could about how the mill works,' he said, ruffling his son's hair affectionately.

Tom started a long explanation of how the mill wheels ground the corn, and Kai, bored, began to wander around, looking out of the windows onto the yellows and reds of the autumn trees that grew along the riverbank. She had her back to the boys when she heard Tom shouting.

'Jack! Stop it! Get back now!' Tom sounded furious. When Kai looked around, she saw that Jack was leaning right into the deep pit where the huge wheel was turning around.

'Come away! You could be caught in the wheel and dragged down there and crushed! You would be killed!' Tom's face was white.

Jack just laughed. 'Oh, Brother Albert says I have nine lives, like a cat!' he said.

'It's not funny,' said Tom. 'One of our apprentices died that way – you can still see the mark of the blood, way down there.'

The children could see that there was a dark stain on the stones, far below. Kai felt a little sick. All of them were silent.

'Can we go to see the puppies and kittens now?' she finally asked.

Tom nodded. 'We will go to see the puppies first. We keep the kittens and puppies in different barns, otherwise there would be war between their mothers!'

Kai felt a great deal better after they went up into the

haylofts and she had taken the warm, furry bodies of the puppies up in her arms to cuddle and stroke. The puppies wriggled in her grasp, but when they moved on to the kittens, they looked at her with blue, milky eyes and sucked on her finger with tiny, needle-sharp teeth. Now Kai was the one who had to be torn away, as it was time to go into the house for supper.

'Edith is still not well enough to get up, but bring your honey cakes into her room and tell her your adventures,' said Tom's mother when they came in.

The three raced upstairs into the chamber, laughing and talking. But they stopped abruptly at the door. Even since this morning, Edith looked much worse. Her skin was a greenish white and she could hardly raise herself on the pillows when she saw them. She did manage a smile, though, and Jack made her laugh telling stories of Brother Albert's despair at Tom's Latin. But before very long Dame Alisoun came in and said they must not overtire her. Edith waved them goodbye feebly as they left the chamber.

Tom's father said he would bring them back to the priory in his cart, as they would never be able to carry all the fruit, acorns and the honey cakes they had been given. 'I hear that Jack has a way with horses, so I'll let him drive the cart,' he said.

Jack looked overjoyed.

'And I have something else for you,' said Tom's mother

to Kai. Tom had been whispering something to her. Now Dame Alisoun held one of the kittens up to Kai. It was the one that Kai had especially liked, a pure black one with one white-tipped paw.

'How would you like to take this one home?' said Dame Alisoun. 'They can eat on their own now, and are ready to leave their mother. This is the one that you liked best, isn't it? She's a pet. We call her Kitty. But you will have to find your own name for her.'

Kai looked at Tom's mother doubtfully.

'What do you think Brother Albert will say?'

'Brother Albert will not mind. He knows very well that my cats are fine mousers. And I hear tell the priory cat has disappeared. Take her, go on.'

Kai took the kitten, hardly daring to believe her luck. A kitten of her own!

Tom's mother laughed as she saw the kitten dig her claws deep into the cloth of Kai's cloak.

'See, she knows she has found her new home.'

Jack was in high spirits, driving the cart back through the darkening evening, and Kai was so happy she felt she would burst if she did not let her happiness out in some way. She suggested that they all sing for Tom's father, but though Tom joined in, his heart was not in it. It was not just that he was sad to be leaving his family. He was also very worried about his little sister. Of all the family, Edith had been the one most full of life and mischief, the one who talked without pause and never stayed still. It was so strange to see her lying so quietly, so pale and silent. His mother had tried to reassure him that Edith would get better, but he had seen how worried she herself looked.

Kai, on the other hand, was in the seventh heaven of delight. She hugged the kitten tightly all the way back to the priory. She had never had a pet of her own before – her family had never been in one place long enough to keep one. Nor had they ever had food to spare to feed even a cat or dog. Despite Tom's mother's reassurances, Kai was still nervous when they got back to the priory and she showed the kitten to Brother Albert. But she found Dame Alisoun had spoken the truth.

Brother Albert laughed and stroked the kitten's head gently.

'That woman knows I have a great fondness for cats myself, and has foisted many of her kittens on me. But in truth they have all been good cats and fine mousers, and as the winter comes in the numbers of rats and mice will increase. So it will be good to have a cat around the kitchens. Though I wish I knew what has happened to poor Quincunx. I fear for him. What will you call this little one?'

Kai hadn't thought of a name yet.

'I don't know. Maybe Blackie?'

Roland's voice came from behind her. As usual, he had

sneaked up to listen into their conversation, without anyone noticing.

'Demon would be a good name! He is as black as Satan – as black as a witch's cat!'

Brother Albert frowned and Roland went away, chanting, 'Witch's cat, witch's cat!'

Brother Albert sighed. Then he smiled at Kai and said, 'Don't pay any heed to him. He is a most unhappy boy. Although from the way he acts, he seems only to want to make himself even more unhappy! I wish I knew what I could do to make him more content and less of a trouble to us all. But now, as regards Madam Kitten, I must tell you that I do not find Blackie very impressive as a name. What about Tertullian? Or Dionysius? They were both Church Fathers.'

Kai looked at him doubtfully.

'They are very long names for a very small kitten,' she said.

'You could shorten it, call her Terry or Dinny, I suppose?' Brother Albert looked so eager that Kai laughed.

'Very well, let's call her Dinny.'

Brother Albert smiled.

'So Dinny it will be. A word of advice though – never leave the kitten alone with young Roland. He has a cruel sense of humour when it comes to animals.'

That night, aware that Brother Albert would not have warned her about Roland lightly, Kai made sure that the door of her cell was tightly shut when she sneaked Dinny into her bed. She did not want her to go missing like Quincunx. In the morning she was woken by the kitten mewing and digging her tiny but amazingly sharp claws into her chest, as if determined to get her up and about in time for lauds, just like Quincunx used to.

Darkness over Dublin

In Kilmainham, the old woman whose job it was to scare away the rooks from the crops had left for her supper. Now the owls were free to fly over the fields, watching for the field mice rustling their way through the grain. One pounce, and it was certain death for the little creatures. But launching itself from its roost into the early moonlight, this owl was disturbed by something strange: an unfamiliar noise. A human. A woman was standing on the bank of the River Cammock, sobbing. The owl stared, its great eyes seeing through the gloom easily. This woman was not part of his kingdom of darkness. Not part of the realm of the hunters, the poachers and foxes and owls and cats, all of those creatures who move invisibly in the darkness and do not wish to be seen or heard. It seemed that this woman did not care who knew she was there. Dame Alisoun was crying as if her heart would break, calling out into the darkness: 'Why Edith? Why my little girl?'

Two days after the children's trip to Kilmainham, word had reached the priory that little Edith had died. There

would be no more coming and going from the mill. The village of Kilmainham had been struck by the plague. Tom was not even allowed to go home for his sister's funeral. When the children sang the service in the chapel on the day she was buried, there was a sense they were singing it for Edith as well as Philip. Dame Maria said as much when they spoke to her after the service. She hugged Tom.

'My poor child, I know it is very hard for you not to be with your family. But from now on, the service you sing will be for your sister too, and for all the lost children of the city. For I fear there will be many more lost to us.'

Dame Maria was right. Almost overnight, the trickle of whispered fears and rumours of strange, sudden deaths became a flood. There could be no denying it now. Plague had come to Dublin, and the city was in crisis. All public gatherings, fairs and markets and guild meetings were stopped. Only religious services were allowed, and these soon became packed out. Hundreds of people came to pray that they and their loved ones should be spared from what soon became known as the Black Death. People flocked in to the cathedral, begging for some holy oil or wax to protect them from the curse of the sickness.

And at the end of September, just after Michaelmas, the weather changed. The sunny autumn days turned to days of unrelenting rain. The Dublin streets became a sea of mud under a sky made of lead. Long days of fuggy mist and constant rain were only relieved by those times when the wind came from the east. But the east wind was harsh and freezing, and it made the rain whip into your face like needles. It cried around the walls of the cathedral like the wailing banshees in the stories that Jack told. And it made everyone depressed.

Tom was trying hard not to cry every time he thought of his little sister. It was so hard to accept that he would never see her again. Kai and Jack tried to cheer him up with plans to raid orchards and explore the crypt under the cathedral, but nothing could keep his grief away for long. And exploring Dublin was no longer such fun. Now, the streets of Dublin were often frightening places to be. The children had seen the parish constable force an old, sick man out of the city gates, because he had the plague and his own family would not let him enter his home.

As for Roland, no one could speak to him without him flying into a rage. There was still no sign of his father coming back to take him home, and each day he hated the priory more and more. Even Brother Albert had moments when he snapped at the children, worn down as he was with his work with the sick. He had stopped most of their lessons until the plague had eased off, for his help was needed all over Dublin.

Kai begged to be allowed to assist him in his work. She was sure her mother's coral would protect her from the disease and she hated to see Brother Albert look so tired and worn and not be able to do anything to help. But Brother

Albert would not allow any of the children to go with him into the disease-stricken houses.

'No, I would not bring you to a house where there are people sick with the plague, but you can help me out in those other houses where help is also needed. It will save my strength and give me more time to work with those suffering worst from this terrible affliction. And you may help Brother Bertrand in the stillroom.' He sighed. 'But I can only do as much as I can do, little enough as it is.'

Kai spent many mornings with Brother Bertrand, who was too feeble to go out to nurse the sick but had taken over Albert's work of mixing the healing potions in the dispensary. Some of the other canons went to visit the sick with Brother Albert. Most often it was Stephen of Derby and Reynalph the Cook who went along with him, but nearly everyone took their turn. Only Brother Malcolm refused point blank to have anything to do with the sick. He did not want the other brothers to go out either.

'We need to keep ourselves in readiness to offer divine service, rather than risk illness. You are placing all of us in danger, carrying foul vapours into the priory. We must keep ourselves pure, free from the contamination of the streets. Those who die from this affliction have no doubt brought God's judgement on themselves.'

Brother Albert shook his head. 'You cannot make me believe that little babies and gentle old men and women have brought plague on themselves as God's judgement. You must surely be able to see for yourself that the disease hits young and old, rich and poor, good and not so good alike.'

But Brother Malcolm was not convinced.

'I'm telling you, if nothing else, this cursed illness is a general judgement on the evil ways of the city. Or perhaps there is some evil lurking within its walls that needs to be routed out.' Here he stared at Kai, as if he thought *she* might be the evil in the city. Probably because she fought so much with Roland, Brother Malcolm had disliked Kai from the day she had arrived at the priory.

He continued, 'And whatever the causes, it seems that the plague spreads very easily. The breath of the dying and the light from their eyes carries it to the healthy. We should all stay safely within the walls of the abbey.'

He left them then and Kai asked Brother Albert, 'Is it really true that the plague can be caught that way?'

Brother Albert said nothing for a moment.

'It is all a great puzzle. It is true that some people believe that the plague is spread by a sick person's breath or by looking in their eyes. But I am not sure they are right. I have seen cases where only one person in a whole household is affected by the disease, although they have all been breathing the same air. Then I have seen others in which the whole household dies. There are different types of the plague, in any case. The most common one is the one that comes on suddenly and leaves the sufferer with buboes – that was the one that took little Edith. It comes on with shivering and fever, and then the buboes, the dreadful black lumps come out on the second or third day. Yet I have seen people recover from this plague, and we cannot say why. The other type of plague seems to sit more in the lungs, and there is terrible coughing and sneezing and spitting blood. That is the worst kind, for the sick person never recovers. It seems to me that the different types must be spread differently, but how, I am not sure. The only thing we do know for certain is that this curse has come upon us because of the Great Conjunction of a few years ago.'

'What is the Great Conjunction?'

'It is when Jupiter and Saturn, the great benefic and the great malefic, are joined together in the sky. It always heralds a disaster of some kind. But though signs and portents may tell us what is to come, they do not tell us how to deal with it. All I can do is pray and do my best to help those who are suffering.'

As the numbers of the dead increased, it became impossible to bury them in holy ground, and graves were dug far outside the city walls, in an area that became known as the Black Pits. Nearly every day the children passed a sad procession carrying some victim of the plague down to this common grave. People in the streets crossed themselves but kept well away from these sad little groups. Very few people wanted to have anything to do with those who had been in contact with the plague. Apart from the monks and nuns, there were few people in the city willing to give any help to those who had been stricken by the illness. As soon as the telltale signs appeared, people who were infected locked themselves in their houses and waited for the end.

But one of those who did try to help was Dame Maria. She and her servant Damaris spent many hours making medicines for the brothers – not just of Holy Trinity but of the other monasteries – to bring to their patients. She asked the children to help her with the distilling of the potions; Roland again refused, as he said it was woman's work, but the others enjoyed the pounding and the pouring and the mixing. Jack wanted to try to make an elixir of life, working away at distilling a mixture of his own invention in one of the retorts in the stillroom as soon as he had finished the tasks Dame Maria set him. His intensity reminded Kai of the time when a friend of her father's had been sure he had a foolproof recipe for turning metal into gold. The Breakwater family had spent months in the alchemist's house, working along with him in his laboratory. The experiments had ended when a large explosion blew up the roof off the house and just avoided blowing the whole family up with it. The alchemist had run around the roofless house with scorched eyebrows, lamenting the ruin of his life's work.

When she told the story, everyone laughed.

Jack said, 'That's the first story I ever heard you tell about your life before you came here, Kai! And it must have been really exciting, with all that travelling. You must have had loads of adventures. Why don't you tell us some more?'

Kai said nothing. She had always been very careful not to talk about her past. She was afraid she might say something to let her secret out.

Dame Maria looked at her face, which had suddenly gone white, and asked, 'Do you think your father will come back to the city soon, Kai? Do you know where he is?'

Kai felt that it was unlikely that her father would come back soon. There were very few people at all coming into the city of Dublin. The city guards were under orders to keep as many people out of the city as they could. It was a way of trying to keep further infection away. In any case, few people wanted to come into a city rife with plague, unless they really had to. She wondered where her father was. She wished now she had not been so mean to him when he had tried to get her to come away with him. In the end, it had turned out that he had been right. The plague *had* come to Dublin.

She said to Dame Maria, 'No, I don't know where he is, and I don't think he will be able to get into Dublin. You know how strict the guards are being about letting travellers in.'

Dame Maria nodded. 'Yes, that's true. And you should be

heading back to the priory, now too, I suppose. Jack, not so fast. You know what you are supposed to do to do when you leave – wash yourself in the rosemary water after handling that waste. You should know the rules of the stillroom by now. Be careful! You will knock over that basin and the stool! Goodness, I never knew a boy to make as much noise as you do!'

Dame Maria was very strict on keeping everything as clean as possible, and urged the children to wash themselves well, even their clothes, having been in the houses of the sick. But even she did not realise that the real cause of the plague was the infection carried in the bites of the fleas that the black rats had brought with them from the east. Those fleas had now deserted the rat population in search of new blood, human blood. Like tiny vampires, they bit into the flesh on men, women and children, infecting their victim, then moving on and leaving them to die.

After they left Dame Maria's house, Kai went to see how Edward was. She had not been able to visit him as often as she would have liked, but she was not worried about him. He still seemed very happy in the stonemason's house. And it had not been attacked by the plague. The only fly in the ointment was Paul, who continued to dislike Edward and never missed a chance to put him down. Kai, visiting her brother in the stone yard one day, had finally lost her temper with the older boy. She turned on him angrily when he came over for the third time to criticise the way Edward held his chisel and worked the stone.

'When you are a master mason, I am sure my brother will be happy to take your advice. At the moment the person he takes guidance from is Master Giles. And Master Giles has nothing but good things to say about his work!'

'Kai, there's no need …' Edward, as usual, was trying to keep the peace.

But now Paul lost his temper too. 'That's enough of your lip, beggar child. We all know you and your brother would both be tramping the roads like your father if the good people of Dublin hadn't taken you in. But I don't see why you spend so much time down here in the stone yard – I hope you are not on the lookout for things to thieve! I must be make sure to check nothing is missing after you leave! It's the likes of you have brought the plague to Dublin, in my opinion. You and your brother should never have been let inside the gates!' He stormed off and Kai was left staring after him with her fists clenched.

Edward put his hand on her shoulder, trying to calm her down. 'Don't let him upset you,' he said. 'I pay no heed to his words, and nor does my master. Everyone else is kindly and makes me welcome, so I ignore Paul as much as I can. But what can I have done to make him dislike me so much? Now come into the house and say hello to Joan. I think she made nut and honey cakes this morning.'

Kai left the mason's house comfortably full of cake, but as she did she was almost run down by a group of chanting, white-clad pilgrims. Some of them were beating themselves on the back with whips as they walked along the streets. The city was full of strange people now – not the jugglers and fairground people of the past, but groups calling out that the end of the world was coming soon, and that everyone must repent or be burned in Hellfire. Processions of these people were seen all over Dublin, shouting out loud about what terrible sinners they were.

Brother Albert snorted when they passed them in the streets. 'Nothing to do with God at all, of course,' he muttered. 'They have just become caught up in some kind of group madness, where they compete with each other to be the most dramatic. Pay no heed to them.'

But Roland's mother had become involved in one of these groups. She came one day to the schoolroom, dressed in a loose white robe and with a crucifix in one hand and a piece of rope in the other. She went over to where Roland was sitting and tried to embrace him. For his part, he had been trying hard to look as if he had no idea who she was.

'My child!' Lady Rachel had a high-pitched, excitable voice. 'You must come with me and tread the path of repentance! Our fair city of Dublin has been polluted with demons and witchcraft! Satan has entered the very gates of the town! We must pray for forgiveness, pray on bended knees, fasting and doing penance, to be saved from the evil that is here amongst us!'

Roland pulled away from her, looking furious.

She must once have been a pretty woman, thought Kai, but she was now so thin and pale that in her white gown she looked like a ghost or, as Jack whispered unkindly to Tom, a banshee.

Brother Albert gently prevented her from dragging Roland out of the room.

'He needs to be here, learning, Dame Rachel,' he said. 'And you know that your husband would not be happy to see him taken away from the priory. Besides, we do not want to lose such a good singer! He is doing God's will here!'

'My husband is a sinner but does not know it! The voices of the saints and the angels told me that! The Lord himself has spoken to me and told me that I am saved and I must bring others to His grace!' Dame Rachel declaimed loudly, still trying to drag Roland from his seat.

Her son's face was so red and he looked so close to tears that the other children felt sorry for him, but did not know what to do, except stay as quiet as they could.

Brother Albert's voice took on a steely note. 'Madam, your husband has left his son in our care. He is as safe from sickness here as he can be in this unhappy city. If he goes with you, he may well catch the disease and we will be answerable to Sir Patrick. Therefore, I must ask you to leave the priory.

If you do not, I will be forced to call for some help to make sure that you do go.'

Lady Rachel dropped her hand and walked out of the room without a word. Brother Albert went over to Roland to see if his arm had been bruised by his mother's grip, but Roland, red-faced and furious, ran from the schoolroom. He kicked the bench where Jack was sitting – and Jack's leg along with it – as he did so. All the children were careful to avoid him for the rest of that day.

But when evening came, Kai came upon Roland in the kitchen. It was pure chance that she was there at all. Sometimes, when they had fish, she couldn't eat her supper, and she often found herself very hungry afterwards. Brother Reynalph would always find something, bread or fruit or nuts, for her if he was there when she went down. But tonight the kitchen was empty, apart from the very sleepy boy tending the fire. Or so she thought, until she saw Dinny flying across the room, letting out a fierce yowl of protest and pain and landing with a thump on the stone floor. Roland was standing at the window, a cruel smile on his face. He had flung the kitten from one side of the kitchen to the other. Kai ran straight at him, pushing him to the ground and shouting, 'How dare you? How dare you? How dare you hurt my Dinny?'

The two of them ended up rolling around on the floor, thumping, biting and scratching each other. Brother Reynalph arrived on the scene and ordered both of them to bed immediately, refusing to listen to either side of the story. He did check that Dinny had not been harmed by her fall, but when Kai tried to tell him what Roland had done he said abruptly, 'I am too tired to listen to you, child. We now have another, terrible worry to contend with. Our prior has been taken ill.'

This was dreadful news. One day Prior Robert had been up and about, his usual hale and smiling self, encouraging his brothers to keep cheerful and busy; the next day he had started to shiver and move restlessly in his bed, and could not bear the least noise near him, or anyone to touch him. By the same evening, he was lying pale and exhausted in the sick-room, unable even to lift a cup of water to his lips. Brother Albert told the children that the plague boils had already appeared under his arms, and smaller boils were also to be found on other parts of his body. The children could hear his cries of agony echoing along the corridors of the priory. Yet he did not die, and the brothers took turns in a constant vigil in the cathedral to pray for his recovery. Roland looked pale when he heard the news and sent yet another message to his father, asking him to get him away from the priory as soon as possible. No answer came.

Next to become ill was Tom. He had been at one of Brother Albert's now very rare lessons, and suddenly fell forward onto the desk. Jack and Kai stared at him in horror. They could see the paleness that heralded the first signs of sickness. Brother Albert lips tightened and he gave a deep sigh. He lifted Tom gently and carried him to the infirmary. On the small white bed, Tom lay tossing and turning.

Jack said furiously, 'You have to let us help look after him. Please. If we are going to be infected we are infected already; it won't make any difference if we are near him.'

Kai nodded, ready to do anything to help her friend. She put her hand to the coral at her throat; her mother's charm would surely protect her. She saw Brother Albert glancing around.

Roland was no longer in the room.

'Roland doesn't want to help,' said Kai stoutly. 'And we are better off without him. I wouldn't trust him to do things properly.'

Brother Albert looked from one of them to the other, and then to Tom, lying pale and restless on the bed.

'Very well. I am at my wit's end trying to look after so many patients. In truth, I do not know how I could do without your help. But you must do exactly as I say. You must be sure to get plenty of rest. And you will need to listen to me very carefully, while I give you your first lessons in care of the plague victims. Keep everything as clean as possible. Touch Tom only when you have too. Keep away from his breath, as the plague is said to spread through humours in the air. Above all, pray constantly. Give him rosewater and sugar, if he can take it without choking. There is very little we can do, except keep him as still and as comfortable as possible. Again, if he can take it in, try to get him to keep down the herbal potions Brother Bertrand and Dame Maria have brewed. And watch and pray, children, watch and pray.'

And that was what Jack and Kai did. They took turns to stay with Tom and nurse him day and night. Kai thought she had never seen Jack so quiet and serious, or work so hard at anything. As Brother Albert was caught up nursing the prior and trying to keep pace with the number of sick people in Dublin, the care of Tom was left mainly to them. On the day after he had fallen ill, the horrible buboes formed under his arms. Black patches appeared on his skin.

They took turns to wipe Tom's forehead and feed him medicines, to change his bedclothes and speak to him, telling him stories and giving as much comfort to him as possible.

It was hard sometimes, to be with their friend and see him in so much pain. They could do so little to help. He would moan and ask for his mother, but his mother was still not allowed into the city to see him. One day, he started to ask for Edith.

'I'm sorry Tom,' said Kai, trying to hold back her tears. 'She can't come either.'

Tom's face broke into a smile.

'But she is here. Can't you hear her, Kai? She *has* come to see me. She's talking to me, teasing me, like she used to.'

Kai did not know what to say. This was really worrying,

to have Tom talk as if he could already speak to the dead. She started to say something, but Tom whispered, his voice cracked and feeble, 'Sssh, Kai, just listen.'

So Kai sat silently, sure that there was nothing to hear but the harsh voices of the gulls flying up from the river outside, and then the bells of St Patrick's tolling the news of another death. She sat for a long time, almost drifting into sleep, but as Tom himself fell asleep, she thought she heard, very softly, the laughter of a girl.

The days passed. Then one day Jack suddenly grasped Kai's hand and said, 'I'm sorry, Kai, I think I've got it too,' and slid quietly to the floor. Now Kai had two patients. But as Jack fell ill, she thought that Tom seemed slightly better, though he was still very weak. Brother Albert said that the fact he was still alive during the days after the boils had formed was a good sign. She tried to divide her time as best she could between the two boys, running from one bed to the other in the infirmary with bowls and cloths and potions until she felt dizzy.

Then there came a night when Tom seemed especially bad, tossing and turning and throwing his blankets off the bed, calling out for Edith and shouting that the mill wouldn't stop turning and was grinding his bones ... that Greenteeth Jenny was there, calling him into the water and that the puca was coming to take him away ...

Brother Albert came and looked serious, but when Kai

asked him what she should do, he said, 'All you can do is keep doing as you have been. And watch and pray, watch and pray.' He laid his hand lightly on Tom's forehead, and closed his eyes as if saying a prayer.

Kai stayed up all that night with Tom. The morning came, and he was still alive, but Kai was asleep on the floor by his bedside, worn out. Brother Albert found her there when he came in to check the children on his morning rounds, and carried her carefully to her own bed.

When Kai woke up, the sun was blazing through the dormitory windows, and she realised it must be almost midday. She ran, panicked, to the infirmary. But there was Tom, propped up on the pallet and trying to smile. She raced over and looked at him closely.

'You are better?'

'I wouldn't say better, but Brother Albert says the worst has passed, and it looks as if I may be one of the lucky ones! I'll have three scars, from all the boils,' he said, his voice weak, but still proud.

'Where is Brother Albert?' Kai looked around and noticed that he was over at Jack's pallet. She was just about to call out the good news of Tom's recovery when something stopped her. She started in horror.

'No,' she said. 'No, it can't be!'

For Brother Albert was drawing the rough linen sheet over Jack's face.

Tom looked over and his own face, already white, blenched even more. He clutched at Kai's arm, but she pulled away and ran to Jack's bedside.

Brother Albert looked at Kai, his face so sad that Kai, even in her own misery, wanted to comfort him.

'I'm sorry, Kai,' he said. 'There was nothing I could do. He has gone to his Lord. Go, get some charred wood from the fireplace, and we will mark the sign of the cross on the sheet.'

Kai did as she was asked, but even as they wrapped Jack carefully in clean white linen, somewhere, very deep inside, she could not believe that he was gone. It couldn't be true. Not Jack, so full of life, so happy all the time. Brother Albert said that the illness had gone on so long it had weakened everything – his heart, his lungs – and he had lost the strength to live. He had died in his sleep while Tom had struggled to stay alive. For once, Jack had managed to leave quietly. Nobody had even noticed him go.

Tom had seen Brother Albert draw the covers over his friend's face and, like Kai, knew what it meant. He turned his face to the wall and said nothing.

Brother Albert came over and laid his hand on his shoulder.

'He is gone to Paradise, child, he is with the Holy Angels and Saints.'

Tom still said nothing. But when Brother Albert left and Kai went to try to talk to him he whispered, 'Never mind the garden of Paradise and the angels and saints. Jack would hate to be surrounded by people who behaved themselves all the time. He is gone to the Elysian Fields, Kai. He is racing his horse there now, a black one with a white star, and he is happy. I'm going to try to think of that when I think of him.'

They were still sitting there when Brother Benedict came in, his face wet with tears. When he saw that Jack had died, he cried out, 'Glory be to the Lord God of Hosts! The two souls have gone together to the Lord! Prior Robert died this morning at dawn!'

Edward Accused

It was a cold clear day in late autumn. The cathedral was filled with the tolling of the bell and the sorrowful voices of the canons. The sadness of the singers seemed to echo in the cathedral, as if other voices were joining in, mourning the loss of the prior and the orphan boy. Kai shivered as she sat with only Roland as company on the bench where the four of them had sung together only a short time before. In the silence between the singing, she was almost sure she could hear the whispers, the muffled voices that she had heard on her first day. There had been other times when she thought she had heard the voices and laughter in the cathedral. As time went on, she heard it more often, and the laughter of the hidden children seemed to be becoming louder, as if more children were joining in. But she told herself that she must be imagining things. Miracles and magic were nothing but tricks and deception.

Now the canons had finished, on a final sombre note, and they filed out of the cathedral. Prior Robert had been

greatly loved by all of them. He had always been fair, had always been kind; had always known what to do in a crisis. He would be badly missed. But as well as being sad, the canons were frightened. There was a buzz of tension in the priory, which seemed new and strange in such a tranquil place.

As Roland and Kai left the cathedral, they noticed Brother Reynaph and Brother Bertrand whispering to each other in the cloister. They stopped abruptly as soon the children came near them. A little further on, Brother Malcolm and Brother Nicholas were also deep in conversation, a conversation which also stopped as soon as they noticed the children approaching. It seemed as if everyone was watching and waiting and listening. But then nothing was normal anymore. Nobody knew quite how to go about the ordinary business of daily life. It was as if, with the loss of the prior, the canons were like sheep without a shepherd. Or, as Roland put it more unkindly, a flock of headless chickens.

Later, Brother Albert explained the air of panic to Kai and Tom, 'It is not just that we have lost a leader that we all loved. Now, we have to elect a new prior as quickly as possible. The king will try to take the priory from us if we are left without a leader for too long. It is the way the law works – the king is the lord of the land and the lands go back to him if they are not claimed. It's ridiculous, but it's the way things are.'

Kai frowned. 'But I don't understand – can't the priory or

the brothers just claim the land? Instead of the prior?'

'No, the land is held by the prior in the name of the priory. It has happened before that the escheator – that's the king's agent – has tried to claim the lands. He can do that if there is too much of a delay in the election of a new prior.'

'But that's so unfair,' said Tom. 'Who is the escheator, anyway?'

'That's one good thing – there isn't one at the moment. Some people say that Roland's father will be the next one. And, at the moment, he's in England. But he is due back at any time. And whoever it is, and unfair or not, that's what the escheator will do. It's his job to try to get as much land as possible for the king. So the election for the new prior will be tomorrow morning.'

Brother Albert sighed. 'And I can only hope that Brother Malcolm doesn't win and become our prior!'

The meeting to elect the new prior was held in the chapter house, after lauds on Sunday. Kai went to the infirmary to be with Tom while the monks met to vote. The two of them sat in silence. They sometimes found it hard to talk to one another since the death of Jack. It was as if there was nothing left to say. Kai wondered if she could have nursed Jack better, and felt guilty because she had not been with him on his last night. Tom wondered if his friend had caught the plague from him.

Brother Albert had tried to reassure them both, saying that there was nothing anyone could have done to save Jack and that the type of plague he had caught was not the same as the one Tom had suffered from. 'And Kai,' he had continued, 'nobody could have worked harder or taken better care of Jack and Tom. And you know, you both gave him a very great gift. When he died, he knew that he was greatly loved.'

That's all very well, thought Tom. But it didn't stop them missing Jack. Looking at Kai's tear-stained face, he decided he couldn't stand sitting like this any longer.

'Let's sneak out and see if we can hear what's happening,' he said. 'I can't bear to stay here looking at Jack's empty bed.'

'But you are still sick and I'm supposed to look after you. And make sure you *do* stay resting,' protested Kai.

Tom snorted. 'I'm fine. I'll feel sicker if I have to wait and hear that Brother Malcolm is the new prior. Imagine how much more obnoxious that would make his pet Roland! He's bad enough as it is!'

They crept out of the infirmary and went to the chapter house. There, they lurked around outside. When they heard the cheer on the other side of the door, Tom put his ear up against it in an attempt to hear what was going on. As a result, he fell over when Brother Albert opened it abruptly. But Brother Albert just smiled.

'Aha, I was just coming to tell you the news. Stephen of Derby is our new prior,' he said. 'And Kai, you are invited to share in the celebration breakfast he is giving in the refectory. Tom, you are going to go straight back to bed. Kai will bring you some sweet things from the table. Well, we can breathe again. It's such a relief. The vote went for Stephen, eleven to two. And that included Malcolm voting for himself.'

'Who else voted for Brother Malcolm?' asked Kai. Brother Albert snorted. 'Oh, Brother Nicholas, of course. But that was just because he has had arguments with Brother Stephen about how to decorate the cathedral. Brother Nicholas has terrible taste. Now, the ceremony to make Brother Stephen prior will be held next Sunday, and Kai, we will have to work hard. We must practise some new pieces for the choir for it.'

'I'll do it happily,' said Kai, thinking of how awful it would have been if they had had to sing for the inauguration of Brother Malcolm. But then she remembered that Jack would not be singing with them. Suddenly the world went dark again.

Before there could be the celebrations for the new prior, there had to be a funeral for the old one. Jack and the prior were buried at the same time, on the eve of All Souls, and the funeral was horrible. Tom was still too ill to come to sing in the choir, though he had fought hard with Brother Albert to be allowed to do so. Kai struggled through the singing with Roland and with two boys from St Patrick's choir dragged in hastily to fill Jack and Tom's parts. They were two boys that they had often had skirmishes with in the streets of Dublin, and the pair of them spent all of the time they were not singing making faces at Kai and Roland. Somehow being angry with them helped Kai through the Mass, but as soon as it was over she ran from the cathedral. It was a wet and miserable day and the streets were full of pig and goose traders, for the Martinmas fair, held on the 11th of November, was coming up soon. All of Dublin smelled of pig and goose droppings. The pigs squealed like the Dolocher and kept getting loose and barging through the streets. Kai's ears hurt. Her head hurt. Her heart hurt most of all. This is what it must be like to be in hell, she thought.

She ran. She knew she should go back to keep Tom company in the infirmary, but the thought of the two of them sitting there without Jack was too much to bear. She didn't know where she wanted to run to, but she finally found herself at the small door in the wall at Giles the stonemason's yard, and she beat on it until her fingers were sore. She really wanted to see her brother, to be enveloped in one of his bear-like hugs. Indeed, she had thought he would have come to the funeral Mass, but he had been nowhere to be seen in the crowd.

The door finally opened, just by a crack. Standing there

was Joan, Master Giles's daughter, her face smudged with dirt and tearstained. Kai's first feeling was one of astonishment. Joan was always very neat and clean in her ways. The girl's face crumpled up when she saw Kai.

'What is it?' Kai asked.

Joan burst into tears.

'I'm sorry, I can't let you in – my father is so angry!'

'What's happened? Where's Edward?'

More tears. Then Joan said, 'Listen, I'm not supposed to go out, but come in for a moment; there's no one in the kitchen. Come quickly so nobody sees you. It's Edward …'

'Is he sick? Is it the plague?' Kai felt her stomach turn over with fear.

'No, nothing like that ... but come in here and I'll tell you …'

The two girls made their way across the yard and into the kitchen. Joan kept glancing over her shoulder, afraid she would be spotted by one of her parents. There was no sign of Edward working in the yard.

In the kitchen, Kai took Joan by the arm and said, 'Now, tell me what has happened to my brother.'

Joan took a breath and began, faltering slightly as her tears overcame her.

'I'm sure it's all a mistake. I know Edward would never have stolen anything. But it was found in his bundle!'

'What was found in his bundle?' asked Kai, with as much patience as she could muster.

'The silver virgin, the one belonging to Dame Rachel. It's a copy of the White Mary of Dublin. You see, she wanted my father to make a stone copy of the statue, so we had it here to copy from it. And then it went missing. So everywhere was searched and my mother found it in Edward's bundle!'

Kai knew her brother. He would never have stolen anything from anyone, never mind people who had been so good to him.

'It must be a mistake – or someone must have put it there. I know my brother would not do such a thing. Is there anyone here that might wish Edward harm?'

Joan shook her head, but Kai had immediately thought of Paul. She said nothing for a moment, just stared at Joan. Joan blushed.

'Maybe Paul. He ... he knows that me and Edward are good friends. And he is always asking me to go out walking with *him*. But I don't like him. I think he might be a bit jealous of Edward. Do you think he could be the one who did it?'

Kai shrugged.

'It's possible, isn't it? That's what we have to find out. But where is my brother now?'

'Oh, my father was furious. First of all he was going to call the parish constable, but then my mother persuaded him that the statue had been found so there was no need for that. But he has sent Edward away. He told him if he didn't get out of

Dublin before nightfall, he would set the Watch on him. So mother and I packed some food for him and he left yesterday. But before he left, he asked me to go to you and tell you that he is going to find your father. I tried to get up to the cathedral, but I couldn't get away from the house. Edward said to tell you that he and your father would come back together and get you. But there is a problem. He doesn't know where your father is.'

'Me neither,' said Kai dolefully. At this point there was noise from outside.

'That's Ymna bringing in the washing. You had better go, Kai. I'll talk to my father about Paul – maybe we will be able to clear Edward's name. And then he can come back and everything will be the way it was.'

Kai left and started to wander aimlessly through the streets. Then something struck her. Ymna! Ymna would know where her father was! Kai rushed after the washerwoman and caught her arm just as she was entering her own house.

They went in together. Ymna's house was full of familiar smells: lye from the soap she made, hops from the brewing house next door; it was steamy and crowded and warm, warm as Ymna's hug.

'Kai!' Ymna dropped her basket and enveloped her in a hug that nearly knocked the breath out of her. 'How are you, child? What have ya been up to at all? I heard you singing in the cathedral – went special, I did, and you sounded like a little angel from heaven. But why haven't you come to see me before now?'

Kai didn't know what to say. She suddenly felt bad. Ymna had always been kind to her, even if her voice was a little loud and she hugged her too tightly and smelled of the harsh soaps she used for her washing.

'I'm sorry. But it's been so busy with all the sickness …' Her voice trailed away.

Ymna, who rarely drew breath to listen to other people, continued, 'Of course, it's been awful. My own sister's husband has been taken … And now there is this terrible business with poor Edward. I have just heard the news. As if Edward would ever steal anything!'

'We must get word to my father, Ymna. He said you would know where he is. Do you?'

Ymna shook her head. 'I'm sorry, child, I have had no word since he left in August. There are so few people coming into the city now. But I will try to find out for you. That I promise you! Don't look so worried! The Lord and his Blessed Mother will look after us. I am sure everything will work out to the good in the end!'

The Voices from the Past

But nothing will really come to the good, nothing will ever be the way it was, thought Kai. She left Ymna's house, refusing her comforting offer of a hot drink and pastries, and as she faced into the bitter east wind, she found that she was crying. She hurried into an alleyway and hid her face against the wood of a doorway. Her father was missing. Jack was dead. Edward was in terrible trouble and had left her alone in Dublin. He might never be able to return. Kai knew that her brother would never have stolen anything from Master Giles. But of course he would be the one to be suspected of the theft. Everyone knew that Edward was the son of a fairground magician. One of those travellers who had no home and must always be suspected of the worst deeds – easy targets for blame when anything went wrong.

Now she had nobody. She thought of going to Dame Maria's house, of letting her hug her and crying on her shoulder. Of telling her about the mess Edward was in. But then

she remembered seeing Dame Maria's face in the crowd at Mass. She had looked as if her heart was broken and she was sure that she was remembering her own dead boy. She had enough sorrows to deal with. And in any case, how could Dame Maria help? Kai had kept too many secrets from her. If she started to tell Dame Maria things, perhaps she would not be able to stop, and all her secrets would come out.

She wandered the streets in a fog of tears, bumping into people and being soundly cursed. Dublin had never felt so bleak and cold and uncaring. At last she found herself back at the cathedral. It was almost evening. The walls towered over her, stern and hard and dark. She made her way in through the entrance of Hell, not caring if the Dolocher came out from the shadows to get her. Then some impulse made her creep through a side door into the cathedral. It was completely empty. The dusk made the nave seem like a cave, or a forest where darkness had come, creating deep shadows among the stone trees. But in here, for some reason the darkness felt not cold, or frightening, but gentle. Comforting. And here she was alone, away from the crowds of people who looked at her and did not care that she was crying. There was no one to see her tearstained face. She went to one of her favourite places, the little chapel where the child's tomb was. She found a place to sit, just beside a pillar carved with oak leaves and little singing birds, and leaned her cheek against the cool stone, caressing it gently. It was very quiet, far away from the shouting of the streets. As she sat, the evening sun broke through the clouds and its rays through the stained glass made rainbow reflections on the stone walls of the church.

She thought of Jack, of how he loved horses and singing. She remembered what Tom had said, just after their friend had died. He will be riding on a beautiful horse and singing his heart out, that's what he'll be doing now, she said to herself. I'll sing for him, she thought. I can't do anything, but I'll sing my part for him. And so she did. She raised her head and sang one of his favourite hymns to the Mother of God, and her voice started small and lonely in the great expanse of stone, but as she sang, it grew louder and clearer. It soared upwards into the stone forest, like a bird rising into the branches of a tree. Under her hand, the stone became warm and felt almost alive, as if there was some force of energy pulsing through it – as if there was a flame lit somewhere deep inside, deep in its heart.

And then, as she sang, the other voices came. They were the voices she had half-heard before, but now they were louder and clearer. They were children's voices and they joined with hers, singing the different parts of the hymn. High and sweet they were, and they filled the cathedral with music. At the end of the hymn, the music faded, echoing back into the stone. Under her fingers the stone became cool and still.

And Kai, though not afraid – for who could be afraid of

those voices? – wondered what could be happening. Was it magic? But she didn't believe in magic. She didn't believe in miracles. Had she gone mad? Well, she said to herself, if she was mad, she might as well ask.

'Who is it?' She called into the depths of the stone forest. 'Who is singing?'

There was a laugh. Laughter with no source. A child's laugh. Could a child be hiding in the shadows? There was something familiar about the sound …

A voice came, a voice so well-remembered, and so full of happiness.

'It's Jack, you nitwit. Or at least it's my voice.'

'But, but, Jack, you're …'

'Yes, I know I'm dead. And all is well, Kai, really it is. There is a part of me very happy riding in those Elysian Fields, now. But there is a part of me here too, in the cathedral, where I was so happy when I was singing. And I'm not the only one. Philip is here too! And you wouldn't believe the number of other children who are here with me and him, who have sung in the cathedral since it was founded, right back to Saint Laurence's time and even before, when the Danish kings ruled Dublin. They have great stories, Kai; you'll have to come back again to hear them. Oh, I wish you could see them all, but it is amazing that you can hear them. Very few people have been ever able to do that, though they have been here all the time. I think it was your singing made a sort of echo in time ... and we were able to become part of it. But you had better go now; you know they are all worried about you in the priory. They have been looking for you everywhere since you disappeared. And anyway the canons will be coming soon to sing their office. But you must come back again, when there is no one else here. And if you sing I will come and join you, and my friends will come too.'

'Of course I'll come. Oh Jack, can I tell Tom and bring him with me?'

'I wish you could. But you must be careful. It is possible that he wouldn't be able to hear us. He isn't like you, Kate, he doesn't have the gift you have, of listening. It's the same with Brother Albert; I could not make him hear. But you must try to let them know that I am so very happy now. And when you are all singing in the cathedral, I'll be there with you too, listening, and content.'

Kai paused. She had suddenly realised that Jack was calling her Kate, not Kai.

'You know who I really am, now, don't you? You know I'm a girl?' she said shyly.

Jack laughed again. 'Of course I do. That's the kind of thing that makes being a ghost such fun!'

Demons in the Crypt and Witches in the Water

The next day Kai told Tom about Edward's flight from Dublin. When he heard what had happened he was as furious as she was. 'I know Paul. He's mean and he's jealous and I'm sure he is the one who put the statue in Edward's bundle. Let's go down to see Joan, and try to make her get a confession out of him.'

They made their way slowly down to Master Giles's house. Tom, still weak, was very pale by the time they reached the door in the wall.

Joan refused to let them in, but she did creep out to talk to them.

'I'm sorry, Kai,' she said. 'My father has told me to have nothing to do with you.

Kai thought hard. It was going to be difficult to get Joan to help. She didn't seem to have the kind of courage or energy

it would take to get a confession out of anyone.

She said, 'Joan, you are going to have to find some way of proving that Paul put the statue in Edward's bundle so he would be blamed for the theft. Talk to him, pretend you think he's clever or something, and try to get him to admit what he has done. You don't believe that my brother stole the statue, do you?'

'No,' said Joan, 'Of course not. But what can I do? I can't force Paul to confess!'

'You are just going to have to be really nice to him for a while. Trap him into saying too much.'

A look of disgust passed over Joan's face. 'But I hate him. He's so hairy and rough and – and stupid.'

Kai sighed, but Tom said, 'Stupid is good, Joan, stupid means that he will be easier to fool.'

After they left Joan, Kai looked at Tom and shrugged. They did not have a great deal of confidence in Joan. Neither was sure she would be able to help them.

Tom said, 'I'm certain that Edward will find your father and all will work out well, Kai. But we must do what we can to help prove he is innocent. Let's keep an eye on Paul and see if he does anything suspicious.'

So, for the next few days, whenever they got a chance, the children made their way down to the stone yard and the house nearby, where Paul had his lodgings. They found that his life was very boring. When he left the stone yard he went straight to the inn, The Black Fox, where he spent most of the evening drinking. On the third day, they were just preparing to go out for their usual surveillance session when Joan appeared at the priory gate, breathless and red-faced.

'He told me,' she said, almost squeaking with excitement. 'He told me he did it!'

'What? When?' Tom and Kai spoke at the same time.

'When we were alone together in the kitchen. He came in and I think he must have had too much ale – he was lucky my father didn't see him. And he seemed to want to talk, so then I gave him cider and sat down with him. He was complaining that no one had any respect for him, so I flattered him like you said, Kai. And then he told me that he was cleverer than my father thought, and how he had hidden the statue in Edward's things. I ran straight out and told my father, but when I came back ...' Joan burst into tears. 'When I came back Paul denied everything. And the worst part is that my father believed him. He said I was just trying to help Edward. But Paul did it, Kai, he even *said* he did it.'

Kai looked grim. She thought for a while.

'So what we need to do is make him confess in front of everyone. Joan, is Paul religious?'

Joan looked puzzled but shook her head. 'He's not, not at all, but he is very superstitious. He listens to stories in the ale-house about creatures like the Dolocher and about the dead rising. He hates working anywhere there are tombs. He is afraid of the idea of dead people being near.'

'Hmm ... and is he due to come to work at Christ Church at all?'

'I don't know,' said Joan, 'but I can find out. What are you going to do? Have you a plan?'

Kai had thought of the voices in Christ Church. If only Paul could hear them! They might frighten him into making a confession. But then something struck her. Perhaps she and Tom and Joan could provide their own ghostly chorus.

'Let me think for a bit. I think we might be able to make Paul confess if he is as superstitious as you say. It's worth a try anyway. We could all hide in the cathedral and *pretend* to be ghosts. It might frighten him into telling the truth.'

Joan looked doubtful. 'I can't sneak off any more and disappear. I can hardly believe I was able to get away today without someone stopping me. I'm a girl, remember. I can't do things that you boys can do. I'm watched all the time and my mother is always looking for me to help her around the house. Anyway, I'd be too frightened to spend ages in the cathedral. It's so big and dark in there.'

She shivered and then blushed. Kai and Tom were staring at her and neither of them looked impressed by her excuses. Kai was thinking how easy it was for Joan. There she was, with her shiny long hair, wearing a beautiful red dress and a pretty necklace and knowing she could just sit back and let Kai and Tom do all the work. All she had to do was say she was a girl. But then she felt bad. Joan had tried her best. And now Joan added, 'But if I can't come to the cathedral at least I'll find out if Paul is due to work there in the next few days, and let you know what's happening.'

The children were in luck. The new prior had been concerned for some time that one of the pillars in the crypt – the oldest part of the cathedral – was damaged. There were loose stones in the pillar, and Prior Stephen asked Giles to send a man up to do a repair job. Paul was chosen. He appeared with a large candle and a nervous expression, not at all pleased at having to go down into the dark depths of the crypt. The children followed him. Kai had already set things up by bumping into him on his way into the priory and giving an exaggerated shiver.

'Oooh, are you going down into the crypt?' she asked. 'I'd never go down there, it's haunted!'

Brother Reynulph, who was with Paul to show him the way, told her sharply not to speak such nonsense, but Kai was happy to see that Paul's ruddy face had turned slightly green.

Paul had left the door at the top of the stairs open, but the children, creeping in behind, closed it with a bang. They had the pleasure of seeing the candlelight flicker and Paul jump. Then they took their positions behind the pillars and waited. They let him take his tools out of his bag, along with a naggin of whisky which he swallowed quickly before he began to chip at some crumbling stone.

Kai let out a low moan.

Startled, Paul dropped his chisel.

Kai moaned again. Tom joined in, whispering very softly, 'Paul, Paul!'

'Who is there?' asked Paul, his voice shaking. 'Who is it? I can't see you!'

'Paul, Paul,' repeated Tom, just about managing to keep the laughter out of his voice. Really, thought Kai, her friend would never make a career out of acting. As Paul strained his eyes to see where the noise was coming from, Kai silently moved up behind him and blew out the candle. Now it was completely dark in the crypt. Paul began to make his way blindly towards the door, his breath ragged with fear. The two children followed him, whispering. 'Paul, Paul,' and then Kai began: 'Confess! Confess! You know you are guilty! Confess or we will cooome for yoooo ...' She let her words end in a moan like the wind's.

Paul scrambled up the stairway, slipping in his panic and hitting his knee hard on the stone. He cursed. Then he screamed. The children screamed too and clutched each other in the darkness. Out of the shadows something pale came hurtling at the stonemason, shrieking like a banshee. Paul lost his mind with fear and screamed again and again. He made it to the doorway and fumbled frantically with the bolt. It finally opened and he fell out onto the ground, almost crying with relief. In the light coming from the open door, the children could see the shape of something white and fluffy sitting calmly on one of the steps that led down to the crypt. It seemed to be positively grinning at them.

'Well, at least we know now where Quincunx got to,' said Tom.

After the trick they had played on Paul, Kai and Tom became closer. But although some part of Kai really wanted to tell him about what had happened to her in the cathedral, she could not force herself to do so. She was afraid he would think she was mad. She remembered how after Roland's mother's visit they had all agreed how peculiar she was, listening to voices telling her what to do.

As time went on, Tom guessed she was keeping something from him, and kept teasing her, trying to find out what it was. They sometimes came near to quarrelling. They both missed Jack very badly, and things were not helped by the fact that Roland was at his most obnoxious, for his father was due to come home soon. He was convinced that he was going to be made justiciar, the highest office in the land.

'Roland is driving me mad,' Tom complained to Kai. 'And you, Kai, you are different, you have been different since ... since Jack died. What's going on? Why won't you tell me? Am I not your friend?'

Kai looked at his hurt face and felt guilty, but if he was not going to be able to hear the voices of the children, how could he believe her? Should she bring him to the cathedral anyway and let him think she was mad? He might even think she was involved in some kind of evil magic. Even though Tom was a friend, settled people almost always believed the worst of those who lived on the roads and survived by their wits.

She said nothing.

'All right then,' Tom said. 'Keep your stupid old secrets.' Really, he thought, his friend was so stubborn. Kai obviously didn't trust him and that hurt Tom very much. He walked angrily away.

Kai felt really bad. Maybe she should have told Tom. Maybe, even if he couldn't hear what she heard, he would have believed her. The problem was, with her, it was always easier to keep a secret than to tell someone what was going on. She had been doing that all her life.

She went back to the cathedral. There was no one else there, so once again she started the song about the Virgin. And again the other voices joined with her and sang with her. And once again when she finished, Jack's voice spoke to her, 'I'm really glad you came back.'

'I'm really glad you did too!'

They laughed, and other voices joined in, laughing.

'Jack, why can't I see you?'

'I don't know. I can see you, and all the others around me. But I don't know if seeing is the right word – I just know they are here.'

'And who is with you?'

'Oh, lots of children. I've made good friends with some of them. There's a boy here you would really like. His name is Finn and he was one of the orphans Laurence O'Toole adopted and gave a home to in the cathedral school. He has great stories about the times he lived in – they had raids and battles and all sorts of things going on then. His best friend is a Danish boy, who was in the cathedral when it was founded, right at the beginning! He was a slave once, and he was brought here by pirates, but he had a wonderful voice so he ended up in the cathedral like us, singing. And there is another boy; he was here the time that Dublin was attacked by Robert Bruce, not so very long ago. The lads have told me everything – about the time there was a fire in Skinner Row that spread to the priory, and everyone had to rush to save the treasures from the cathedral before it burnt down. And how the steeple blew down once, in a storm! That was really frightening.'

'And they all sang in the cathedral, through all those times, didn't they?'

'They kept singing all through the dark times. The cathedral was their shelter. It always protected the people of Dublin, especially children, and the sick and poor and all those who really needed help. There has been a church here for so long, and people have prayed here and sang for so long, it's as if the feelings they left behind have somehow got into the walls, into the stone. The walls have soaked in all the hope and faith and love and goodness. Does that sound stupid?'

Kai thought for a moment.

'No, I think I kind of understand. It's as if the cathedral is like the boat Brother Albert talked about, holding things safe.'

'Yes, like the boat, but like the sea too, or a part of it. Did you ever hold a shell to your ear? You know that way that you can hear the waves? You can hear it singing, as if it was holding the sound of the whole wide ocean. That's what the cathedral is like. It holds a little part of the big sea.'

Secrets and Spies

om was very lonely. He missed Jack badly. He was so fed up sometimes, that he found himself spending time in the company of Roland, something he would never have dreamt of doing a month before. He wished with all his heart that he could be back at home with his family in Kilmainham. But the plague stopped any movement between the village and the city. When he thought of his mother mourning little Edith he felt as if his heart would break. And he wondered what might be happening out there in the mill. Perhaps someone else in his family had got sick and the news had not reached the priory. He prayed every day that the plague would not spread to his mother and father or his other sisters and brothers. He missed them all so much. And he missed Kai too, even though he was still at the priory. But his friend never seemed to be around now. In fact, it almost seemed as if Kai were trying to avoid him. So many times, Kai disappeared off on his own, refusing to say where he was going or what he

was doing. Tom suspected he was going to meet his father, and he was afraid one day he would wake up and find that Kai had gone away completely. Then he and Roland would be left in the priory, just the two of them. It didn't bear thinking about.

So he set himself to watch. But Kai seemed to have a sixth sense about being watched. Any time Tom followed his friend, he would find that Kai was going to Dame Maria's or somewhere else equally innocent. It didn't help that Brother Albert didn't want him to leave the priory; he fussed over him all the time, even though Tom himself knew he had completely recovered from the plague. He just wanted to get back to the mill. He tried to talk to Kai about his longing to get back home:

'With all the sickness in the village, they will need me there. I should be there to help my father. Would it be alright with you if I left the priory?'

Kai looked at him in shock.

'What do you mean? You can't do that and leave me alone with just Roland!'

'I want to help my family run the mill. I think I should go back. My family are there.'

Tom is so lucky, thought Kai. At least he knows where his family is. She had had no word from her father or Edward since the night her brother had fled from the city.

'I can see why you want to go – but please, please don't go

yet. It's already so lonely without Jack.'

'But you are never around anyway. You sneak off and you don't tell me where you are going.'

Kai was silent. Then she drew a breath and said, 'Tom, do you remember when you were sick? Do you remember how you talked to Edith?'

Now it was Tom's turn to be silent. He did vaguely remember the feeling that Edith had been close by him, talking to him, but that must have been just his fever. He didn't even want to think about it. Only mad people heard voices. And why was Kai asking about that now? Was he just trying to change the subject?

He said, 'I don't know what you are talking about, Kai. Roland's mother is the only person I know who hears the voices of people who are not there! And we all know she is a crazy woman. You are so strange, sometimes, Kai. Now, are you going to tell me where you go off to, or not?'

Kai sighed. She had thought that perhaps if Tom remembered Edith he might be able to believe what she told him about the voices in the cathedral, perhaps even be able to hear them. But it was hopeless. There was no point trying to make Tom understand. She didn't want to be thought of as mad, or worse, as some kind of witch. To be accused of magic could mean that you would end up in a court, with the threat of torture or even death hanging over you. She was so tired of being told she was strange. Strange because of her strange name. Strange because she was a stranger. Strange because when she was acting as a boy she seemed girlish. Strange because during those times when she had been allowed to be girl she had been so used to acting as a boy she had been boyish. Strange for too many reasons.

She started to speak but was interrupted by a noise behind them. They had not noticed Roland sneaking up to where they sat talking on the wall by the river. He had been listening in to their conversation.

'Tom speaks the truth. You do sneak around. I've seen you too. Do you go off and do magic with your familiar, that demon cat?'

Kai, tired and frustrated, decided that this evening she was not going to sit and listen to Roland's malicious words.

'Oh stop with your rubbish,' said Kai. 'If you won't be quiet, I tell you, I will push you into the river, I swear I will. Look, there's duckweed, just there. Greenteeth Jenny must be lying in wait. I'm sure I can hear her calling!'

Tom gave Kai a strange look and Kai wondered if she had gone a bit far. She hoped he wouldn't think she really could hear the voice of the spirits in the water – or perhaps even summon them up. She also felt that she was being a little too mean to Roland as she knew that he was really terrified of Greenteeth Jenny. But she was tired of him creeping around and listening in when it was none of his business.

Now Tom took up the tease.

'Greenteeth Jenny, down in the dark waters of the Liffey. She will catch you as soon as look at you and pull you down into the sludge and the slime.'

Kai had mercy. Roland was looking very pale.

'Oh Roland, don't be silly. You know that Greenteeth Jenny is a story for the superstitious, to frighten people.'

But now Roland had become angry.

'No she is not. We all know that there is evil magic out there. And you seem to know an awful lot about spirits and ghosts and witches – an awful lot.' Roland stared at Kai hard as he said this, as if he knew something she didn't. He went on, 'Sorcery is everywhere, and demons are always out to get us if we are not protected from evil. My father …'

The children exchanged glances – not another story about Roland's father!

'My father has been involved in witch hunts in the king's court, and he knows all about the evil things they can do. He has told me all about them. They use cat's blood and cut up …'

'Stop it!' Kai put her hands over her ears. 'We don't want to hear your horrible stories,' she continued, though Tom looked as if he might have listened.

Now Kai noticed that Tom was looking at her as if he was surprised at her reaction to what Roland was saying. She said quickly, 'It's just that I've seen horrible things done to people, because they have been suspected of being witches or sorcerers.' Her voice shook as she remembered what she had seen.

'We were in Chester once, and there was this old woman there, that we had met in the market. She was very cranky and she had a big wart on her nose and nobody liked her. The children used to tease her and she had a stick that she would shake at them. She wasn't a nice old lady at all, but she didn't deserve what happened to her ... Anyway, it seems one of her neighbours got it into her head that the old woman had cast a spell on her cows. They wouldn't give milk. And she had the old lady, Maggie was her name, she had Maggie brought up before the court. I saw her being dragged out of her house and being pricked and prodded in front of everyone. You could see that she was really terrified. My da tried to help her, but then *he* ended up being brought up before the court. In the end he got off, but the old lady was held in a freezing, filthy prison while she was waiting for the trial and she died there. It was dreadful.'

Tom said nothing. He was afraid if he said anything sympathetic Kai might cry, and he knew his friend would hate to show himself as weak in front of Roland. Roland himself merely raised an eyebrow as if something had suddenly clicked into place in his mind. Kai stood up and began to walk away, determined to find somewhere where she could cry in secret. She would never forget that horrible time in Chester, the fear that her father would be imprisoned or worse, the cruelty people had shown to the poor old woman. They had gathered in the streets and screamed again and again 'Kill the witch!' as she was being dragged to prison.

From what she had heard, it seemed typical of Roland's father to have been involved in a witch hunt. He sounded like the type who knew he was always right and loved to catch out other people doing wrong. Just so he could lecture them and punish them and feel completely virtuous about inflicting pain and humiliation on other people. Just like Roland, in fact. At least people like her father, tricksters though they might be, did not stand on judgement on other people.

But Roland couldn't let it go. He shouted after Kai, 'The woman probably *was* a witch! And we all know that your father is involved in some strange things too – magic and the like! He certainly has more than one trick up his sleeve! How else did he manage to win all that money from the sheep farmers last August? Oh, you didn't know that I knew about that, did you?'

Kai said, 'I'm not listening to any more! Let me go!'

For now Roland had caught up with her and was pulling at her sleeve as she tried to walk away.

He began pushing her, saying, 'You should listen to me when I speak! You have no respect for me! I tell you, you will be sorry when my father gets here!'

Kai hated to be pushed, so she pushed back. Perhaps it was

because the push was a little harder than was necessary, or perhaps it happened just because the ground near the river was very muddy and slippery. For whatever reason, there was a scream and Roland slid into the green slime that covered the river. Tom and Kai looked at each other and burst into shocked laughter. But now Roland was screaming that he couldn't swim. The river was deep at this point, and Roland was out of his depth, and already becoming tangled in the green river weed.

'Here, catch my hand,' called Kai, but by now Roland had been pulled away from the shore. Kai and Tom kicked off their shoes and dived in. It was a difficult job to get Roland back to shore, mainly because in his panic the boy kicked and hit out at the two children who were trying to save him. But they finally crawled onto the bank, and lay gasping there, Kai trying hard not to think of the trouble they would be in when they went back to the priory soaked, with their clothes covered in mud.

Roland was the first to pull himself upright. He stood looking down at Kai, his face full of fury.

'You tried to kill me,' he gasped. 'You can be sure I won't forget that. You are evil, like your father, like your thieving brother, like all the vagabonds who bring trouble and disease to Dublin.'

But by the time he had finished speaking Kai was already gone, racing towards the priory to get out of her wet clothes.

Roland raced after her. Tom was left alone on the riverbank, thinking of a time when the three of them – Jack and Kai and himself – would have sat there giggling at the sight of a sodden Roland making his way home, his fine clothes ruined, his fur hood lost in the slime that covered Greenteeth Jenny's bed.

Cat's Eye View

Quincunx kept an eye on what was going on in the priory, though he had moved his quarters to under the vaults of the crypt. Roland had become far too clever at catching him if he hung around the priory kitchen, and although Quincunx missed the scraps, the warmth and the occasional cuddle that he had had access to there, he had a strong sense of self-preservation and knew he was safer away from human sight. He still managed to forage through the scraps from the kitchen, but he had developed quite a taste for the rats that lived in the crypt. He had also found a large chest that had been left carelessly ajar, and nestled down every night in a bed of fine lace and lavender-scented, embroidered linens that were being kept safe for the arrival of important visitors.

He had noticed Kai coming to the cathedral almost every day when no one else was there, and had heard the echoes in the stone, the singing and the voices. The curiosity of cats had brought him to watch her, but went no further than that.

Today however, he noticed someone sneaking in behind her. The hairs on his back rose. It was Roland.

Kai was helping Dame Maria in the quiet of the still-room, one of her favourite places in the city. There, and in the cathedral with the voices around her were the only places she felt safe from the waves of fear and sorrow that had engulfed Dublin. It was terrible how hopeless everyone felt. Myrrh and herbs and verjuice were used to try to help the plague victims, but nothing seemed to make any difference, although they did sometimes seem to ease the agony of those who were dying. And lavender and rosemary water, much less expensive and easier to obtain, did that just as well. In Dame Maria's stillroom, they made vial after vial of those mixtures, pouring the ingredients from mysterious earthen bottles full of essential oils and rosewater and grinding and mixing in herbs and roots.

The room smelled clean and fresh and pure. Kai sometimes longed to live in a house like Dame Maria's, to be part of this clean and orderly world. The priory was clean and very orderly, but it was also rather comfortless and masculine. The canons did not care for decoration, except for in the church. And Kai deeply loved beautiful things: the sheen of an oak table, the glint of light on a well-shone silver cup.

Nobody in the priory seemed to share her need for that particular kind of beauty. Brother Albert found beauty in music and in the words of the psalms, and did not care much about bodily comfort. The person closest to sharing her love of beautiful things was Prior Stephen. He was himself an artist, and he talked of one day, when the bad times were past, commissioning a hymn book that would be a work of art, worthy of the songs that were contained in it. It would be decorated and illustrated in the most beautiful colours. But even in Prior Stephen's case beauty was a song of praise to the glory of God, not something to be treasured for its own sake.

Kai cared about beautiful things simply because they were beautiful. Almost as much as she cared about having order around her. She had had far too much disorder in her life. And she had also had too much of people watching her, suspecting her of something. She hated the fact that Tom had started to spy on her. And Roland had been watching her from the first day she had arrived in the priory. Now he seemed to be constantly spying, trying to find out where she went to during the long periods she spent with the voices in the cathedral. He also never missed a chance to make some horrible comment about her or her father. He himself was ecstatic because his father was due home any day, and he was sure that he would bring with him the news that he was to be the new justiciar. Then he, Roland, would be taken out of the priory to a fine new home in Dublin Castle. One afternoon, he came to choir in new clothes, swaggering into the church.

Tom and Kai put their hands over their mouths, trying to stifle their giggles. He looked ridiculous. It was like nothing anyone had yet seen in Dublin. Roland was dressed in parti-coloured tights of yellow, green and purple, with a red doublet and a purple hat with a yellow plume.

'Can you just imagine what Jack would have had to say about that outfit?' whispered Tom and the pair of them subsided into giggles, and were soundly scolded by Brother Albert. But after the service, Dame Maria smiled too when they spoke to her about Roland's clothes.

'A popinjay, like his father,' she said briskly. 'And no sense of the decorum of colours.'

'Do you know Roland's father?' asked Kai.

'Yes I did. We grew up together, and a more unpleasant little boy I have never met.'

She continued, 'We used to call him Sebastian, because Sebastian was the patron saint of cantankerous children; he was always mewling and complaining and telling tales to our elders, especially if he thought it would get us into trouble.'

'I can't imagine you doing anything bold,' said Kai shyly.

Dame Maria laughed. 'I was a demon, and I got poor Albert – yes, he grew up with me too – into so much trouble. He would never have thought of half the mischief on his own. I hung around with boys until I was forced to grow up. But they were happy days! My husband was one of the gang too and a great friend of Albert. We had such good times!

'I think I was especially wild, because I was a little jealous of the other three. They all sang in the choir, you see, and I wasn't allowed, because I was a girl. I was so jealous – I loved to sing. You have no idea how hard it is not to be allowed to do things that you want to do, just because you were born the wrong sex!'

'Don't I though?' thought Kai wryly, saying nothing. If Dame Maria only knew how much she wanted to know more about making simples and how she made the lovely tapestries on the walls. She could never ask, because it would not be at all natural for a boy to be interested in such things. On several occasions already, she had almost tripped herself up with her interest in things a boy would be unlikely to find fascinating. When she had asked about making beeswax polish, Dame Maria had looked at her quizzically, but she had quickly covered up with a story about Brother James wanting to know the recipe. 'I told him about the way you keep the wood in your house so beautiful.' Then Dame Maria had cheerfully shown her how to mix the beeswax and pine resin with flax seeds and distilled lavender flowers for the recipe.

Now she asked Dame Maria, 'Why is Roland so angry all the time? He hates me, and I don't know why, really. I didn't do anything to him, yet from the beginning he has been horrible to me. And poor old Dinny has to run away him from all the time.'

'Roland is a difficult boy, hard to like. But much of that is because of his parents. His mother you have seen – she is a strange woman, always involved in some enthusiasm or other. Before she became mixed up with that group of very strange people she was mad into some other fad. She has never had much time for Roland. That is one of the reasons he is in the priory. His father could not be sure that she would look after him properly while he was away in England. And Roland's father has been away a long time. In fact, he is hardly ever in Dublin, and when he is, he is very hard on the boy. Roland worships his father; he loves and admires him, but he cannot ever meet his expectations. He does not have the brains of a lawyer like his father nor the courage to be a soldier. I think that is why he is so sour and bitter all the time. Though in fairness, other people have had harder backgrounds and do not end up like him. Look at poor Jack, for example.

'Jack was an orphan, wasn't he? What about him?'

'Yes, he was an orphan, and his past was a hard one. Yet he had no bitterness in him. He was one of the happiest boys I have ever known.'

'Yes he is,' said Kai, thinking of Jack's seemingly endless optimism.

Dame Maria looked at her, puzzled by her use of the present tense and Kai said hastily, 'Do you think it is to do with the humours? Is it because Roland is choleric?'

Brother Albert had given them a lecture on the humours one day. Jack and Tom had slept through it, made drowsy by the autumn sunlight that drifted through the windows, but Kai was enthralled at Brother Albert's descriptions. The melancholic, the sanguine, the choleric and the phlegmatic; Kai loved the words and the fact that it seemed to put some order on the confusing fact that people were so very different.

Jack and her father, she decided, were sanguine, not a care in the world, always sure that things would turn out well. Dame Maria had a large melancholic streak. Edward was phlegmatic, gentle, quiet, waiting for the world to move rather than trying to make it move himself. Tom had a large dose of phlegmatism too. She could not quite be sure what she was herself, but Roland, she had thought, as she watched him squash a drowsy autumn bee under his slate, was definitely choleric. Always ready to take on the world in a battle, even if the world itself did not really want one. Why did he have to kill that bee? What was it that drove him to destroy everything in his path?

Now Dame Maria sighed.

'Perhaps it is that – but then I have known people with the same kind of temperament who have used it to the good. And how is it decided what humours we are given out when we are born? It is all a great mystery, Kai. But although I know Roland is difficult, I do feel sorry for him. He never seems to be happy.'

As there was still no news about her father and brother, Kai decided to visit Ymna, to see if she had managed to find out where her father was. Perhaps she could tell her where Edward was too. When she arrived at the wash-house, Ymna, her arms red from the water, gave her her usual hug.

'There now, my dear. You've got so thin. Those old monks musn't be feeding you at all. But tell me, my honey, have you heard any word from your father?'

Kai shook her head.

'That's what I was going to ask you,' she said. 'I thought you might have heard something about where he is. Or where Edward is too.

'Nothing. My people have had no word of either of them. I only hope your father is not in any trouble.'

Kai could not help smiling.

'He's always in some kind of trouble, Ymna. He's never happy unless he is.'

'I'll send word out again that we need to know where he is. But don't be worrying too much, lass. Ned is like a cat, he always lands on his feet.'

But on her way home Kai could not help but worry about her father. It was all very well to say that Ned Breakwater always landed on his feet, like a cat, but even a cat had only nine lives. Jack had been like a cat too, and his lives had run out. She couldn't bear to think of never seeing her father again. For all she knew, she could even be an orphan, like Jack.

Back within the comforting walls of the cathedral, Kai asked Jack about what it had been like to be an orphan.

'It wasn't so hard, really, once the canons took me in. Before that, I can just about remember Richenda, the woman I was with in Dublin. I was often cold and hungry and dirty, though I remember her giving me a sweetmeat once. But once I was in the priory I felt safe.

'It was the same with so many of the children here – they were orphans too, and Laurence the Bishop brought them here, boys and girls, and looked after them. He kept them in his house, and then when there were too many he boarded them out in families in the city.'

'Tell me some more about St Laurence,' said Kai.

'He was a great bishop, and he tried to make peace between the Normans and the Irish, after Strongbow had invaded Ireland. You know that Strongbow is buried here too, don't you? And St Laurence was the one who brought the Augustinian monks to Christ Church. But the main thing people remember about him was his kindness. And he was really holy. He could hear the voices from the past too; every morning after the first prayers he would go alone to the graveyard and talk to the blessed ones lying there. And he loved music.'

The bell tolled, filling the cathedral with sound, and Kai jumped. 'I'd better go now. I'm going to be late for supper.'

Later, as they ate their pickled herring that evening, Brother Albert shivered and complained that his joints were beginning to ache, a sure sign that the winter was going to be a hard one. There was already frost on the ground and the wind was from the north and bitter.

'But your joints ache every winter,' said Brother Percival.

Brother Albert just laughed and said, 'You speak the truth, but I tell you that the winter will be hard one, believe me or not as you wish. You are not eating your herring, Kai.'

Kai moved the pieces of the herring around on her trencher in an attempt to make it look smaller.

Tom said, 'We have had herring every day this week. If I see any more salted fish, I'm going to throw up. And I hate the way herring bones stick in your teeth.'

'We should be thankful to the Lord. There is many a poor person would be grateful for such a meal.'

Kai made an effort to swallow the fish. 'It's just that I hate eating anything that looks back at you while you are eating it,' she said, carefully covering the fish's head with a bit of boiled onion.

'You really are as picky as a girl,' said Roland. 'I shall begin to call you a girl's name, Margaret or Nan or Kate.'

Kai jumped and felt herself blush. Then she stuck out her tongue at him.

But Tom was quick to defend her. 'Don't you call Kai girlish, he has far more courage than you have. He's the one that will walk the highest walls or go out furthest on the river. Further than you ever would. I think you are still afraid old Jenny Greenteeth will rise out of the water and bite you every time we go near the Liffey.'

'Jenny Greenteeth got Dame Maria's son Philip, didn't she?' said Roland.

'Philip just drowned. It happens,' said Tom.

Kai said, 'I don't care what names you call me. I know who I am and I don't care what your opinion of me is.'

'When my father is back you had better care, for I know there is something strange going on with you and he will find out what it is!'

Brother Albert started to intervene, but Kai lost her temper. 'Don't you threaten me, Roland Fitzhugh, or I swear, I swear, I will make you very sorry you did!'

Roland stood up and was shouting, 'I heard you – you all heard him – he's threatening me! If anything should happen to me, you are the witnesses. If any ill befalls me, it is because he has cursed me!'

After this argument Roland watched Kai even more closely. From the beginning he had suspected that there was something very suspicious about the newest chorister. He was so very secretive – never washing or dressing with the other boys, going off on his own whenever he got the chance. He had spotted Kai sometimes touching something that hung around his neck under his clothes and Roland wondered if it was some kind of magic amulet. He had also heard that witches and warlocks sometimes had a peculiar mark on their bodies, the mark of the devil – perhaps that was what Kai was trying to hide from his companions!

Kai's recent strange behaviour had only strengthened his suspicions. He thought that Kai might be meeting his father, the trickster who had been driven out of town. Or perhaps his brother, the criminal. Roland had made it his business to find out everything he could about Kai's family. He could hardly wait for his own father to come back to Dublin, so that he could tell him his suspicions. In the meantime, he spoke to Brother Malcolm about them, but Malcolm was in a terrible mood as a result of losing the election as prior. It was only when Roland suggested that perhaps his father, as justiciar, might be able to do something about the result of the election that he became enthusiastic.

'I am sure that the canons were under some kind of malign influence when they voted,' said Malcolm. 'If we could show that we could have the election declared illegal and I could be prior.'

Finally, the message came that Roland's father would arrive

back in Dublin within the week. He had been entrusted with an important message from the king; a parliament was to be called to hear it in the castle of Dublin. Lady Rachel left off her penitential robe and dressed herself in jewels and satin in preparation for his arrival. Roland was given permission to go home for a few days, although he would be needed to sing in the great Mass that was being held in the cathedral for Martinmas. Before that, his father arrived, along with a retinue of servants to take his son home from the priory.

Patrick Fitzhugh was disappointing to look at. He was a small, stout man with a wizened face and cold blue eyes. He came back with the news that he had not been made justiciar at all, but instead had been given the post as the new escheator, which was a huge let-down for him. And for Roland.

'Escheator, cheater,' said Tom mockingly. They had all become very tired of hearing about Roland's father. 'Your father is just a thief by any other name, and has only got where he is by flattering the rich and powerful and trying to get other people into trouble. You needn't be so proud of him.'

'And your father? What is he but a jumped-up peasant, a miller? Everyone knows how dishonest millers are. As for Kai – why, his father was run out of town as a beggar and a trickster – a seller of fake potions and medicines, a liar and a rogue. We don't even know where he came from.'

Kai tried to speak, to tell Roland exactly what she thought

of him, but Tom, usually so quiet, had gone very red and his words came out in a rush. He was so furious he would not let Kai get a word in. 'My father is a good man and an honest one. He has never cheated anyone in his life. Our weights are honest and we don't overcharge like some millers, even when the times are hard. He does an honest day's work which is more than can be said about some people.'

'My father works very hard. He is determined to weed out the evils that have brought plague upon Dublin. He has great knowledge and experience in hunting out the devil, and he will do it here.'

'Oh pleeease,' said Kai.

Tom pulled Kai to one side. 'Let's get away from this. Do you want to go down to the river? We could go across to Oxmantown,' he said.

'Not now. I'm sorry, perhaps tomorrow?'

Kai had not been able to get to the cathedral on her own for three days and she desperately wanted to hear from Jack and her other friends. As a result, she was not quite as careful as she might have been when covering her tracks. Tom saw her sneak into the side door of the cathedral. He was just about to follow her when he was spotted by Brother Albert and dragged off to help carry food to some of the poor in Dublin. But on the way, they passed Roland.

A couple of weeks before, Tom would not have dreamed of giving Roland any information about Kai's whereabouts.

But he was angry at being rebuffed once again. So when Roland asked, 'Have you seen Kai?', he replied, 'He's probably in the cathedral, that seems to be where he goes to spend all his spare time.'

And so Roland made his way to the cathedral, where he crept in as quietly as he could and found Kai seated on one of the benches, singing.

But as he sat there, Roland realised that there was something very strange going on. For very faintly, so faintly that Roland could half convince himself it was no more than the wind crying outside the cathedral walls, it seemed that other voices were joining in with Kai. The voices were young voices and seemed to come out from the stone of the walls of the church.

Roland felt the hair on the back of his neck rise. Demons. The boy was communicating with demons.

When the singing had finished, Kai said quietly, 'Thank you. Thank you all. It's so good to be able to sing with you. With friends who know everything about me. I don't know how long more I can go on like this, keeping secrets from everybody.'

There was a noise like a whisper of wind through the church, and then Kai said, 'The worst? The worst is hiding that I'm a girl all the time.'

Roland gasped so hard he almost fell off his seat, and Kai jumped up and looked around her, but Roland had already run from the cathedral. So that was it. Kai was a girl. A girl. If she was a girl and she was talking to demons, she was a witch. He ran until he reached the calefactory, where Brother Malcolm was seated, counting money.

Gasping, Roland stood before him, his brain in a whirl. A female, singing with the holy brothers in Holy Mother church. What sacrilege! And a witch at that, talking to those demons and singing with them. Now it all fell into place: the girlish squeamishness, the black cat, the disease that had arrived with Kai, the fact that he – no she – herself had never been infected by the plague, despite all the time she had spent nursing the sick.

'What is it, boy? What's the matter?' Brother Malcolm was irritable and impatient. Since he realised that Roland's father was not to be made justiciar, he had much less time for the boy.

'It's Kai, brother. I found him – her – in the cathedral. Kai is a girl. And she was singing …'

'What? What nonsense is this? This isn't possible. You were dreaming, boy.'

'I swear I'm not. And, and there were other voices singing with her, demons and monsters. And she said – she talked to them, and she said she was a girl.'

'Are you totally sure about this, boy? Start at the beginning and tell me everything.'

Roland stuttered out what he had seen and heard. He

ended by saying, 'So, we must go and tell the prior, mustn't we, and get her out of the cathedral? She has no right to be on the altar and sing with us. No right to learn Latin and be in the same place as the holy brothers. She must be evil; she must be got out of here. And punished.'

Brother Malcolm looked thoughtful.

'Hmm... no, wait. I am not sure that telling Stephen of Derby is the right way to go about this. He is so meek and mild he will not take strong action. No, this is a terrible crime, and a great danger. We have a witch child in our midst and we must do something about it immediately. You know the punishment for blasphemy as well as witchcraft is burning. There was an Irishman burned for blasphemy on Hoggin Green, not so very long ago.'

Brother Malcolm's brain was working fast. If this story could be made a public scandal, he could make the scandal work in his favour. Imagine, the good brothers of Christ Church harbouring a girl in their midst – a girl who seemed to have magical powers. There would be uproar in Dublin. Perhaps the disgrace would force the prior to resign ... And then there would be space for a new prior, someone untainted. It would be a good excuse to get Brother Albert out of the priory too. To send him off somewhere in the west. Or the east. In any case, somewhere far, far, away.

'I think it best to tell your father. He will do what is necessary – arrest the girl and have her tried. Let us go right away.'

'But will she not need to be tried by the Church?' asked Roland breathlessly as they hurried towards his father's house in Skinner's Row. He knew that that was the usual process for heresy, blasphemy and witchcraft.

'Not necessarily. In fact, I think we may dispense with the idea of a court altogether. If she has to go to trial, who knows how much time she will have to bewitch and bewilder the populace. A straightforward people's court will do, and a fire built close to the High Cross. For her and her cat. That will rid us of this pestilence quickly and cleanly.'

Witch Hunt

As she was leaving the cathedral, Kai had the strangest sense that there was something wrong. Dinny, who greeted her at the door, felt the same way. She rubbed against her, crying anxiously. Kai picked her up and hugged her, wondering what the strange noise was that she had heard in the chapel. The wind? It was windy enough outside, a freezing wind bringing a freezing rain that cut into her face as she made her way across the cloister garth.

She was looking for Tom. She was determined to make it up with him. Even if it meant she had to tell him her secret, she would take the risk. She would have no more secrets from him. He was a friend, after all, and with true friends you were honest. And if they were true friends, they would help you out when you were in trouble. But there was no sign of him anywhere; he must still be with Brother Albert. She felt restless, unable to decide what to do. Perhaps she would go to Master Giles's house and see if Paul had confessed or

Joan had any luck convincing her father that Edward had not stolen the statue. She made her way through St Nicholas's gate and down towards St Kevin's quarter, where the mason's house was.

But as she passed the alleyway that led past St Patrick's towards the Archbishop's Palace and St Kevin's Street, her skin began to crawl. She knew that feeling from her years on the road with her father: the feeling of danger. Someone was watching her, with no good will towards her. Was it the choir boys from St Patrick's lying in wait for her? But she had only time to sense the presence of danger before everything went black.

A sack had gone over her head and shoulders and she was dragged, kicking and screaming, through a doorway and down some foul-smelling narrow stairs. Her hands and feet were tied and then a rope went around her waist and she was attached firmly to a chair. The sack was pulled roughly from her head, and caught the thin chain that held her coral. It broke, and her mother's charm fell to the ground. Looking around her, Kai realised that she must be in some kind of cellar. It smelled of rat droppings and damp. There in front of her was the escheator, along with Roland and Brother Malcolm. They were seated at a table, and Brother Malcolm had parchment and a pen. There was a lantern hanging beside her so that the light shone into her eyes, but apart from the rushlight beside Brother Malcolm's writing materials, their faces were in shadow. Even in the dimness, though, she could still see that Roland had a wide grin on his face and was twitching with excitement.

'Well now,' said Sir Patrick. 'A coney well trapped. First, we must tell you that we know everything – all about your crimes and your witchcraft. But we need some answers from you before we bring you before the people for trial. It will be best for you to confess all to us and to the Good Lord.'

'Confess what? I have done nothing wrong!'

Brother Malcolm broke in, spluttering in his rage. 'Nothing wrong? You have defiled God's altar with your female presence! You have lied to all the holy canons! You have been seen conversing with demons in the very cathedral itself! And who knows what else you have done? Perhaps you are the very cause of the plague that has afflicted us. Perhaps you even swayed the minds of the brothers to vote that feeble cleric, Stephen of Derby, as prior. Nothing wrong indeed!'

The escheator cast a disapproving glance at Brother Malcolm.

'That is no way to place the charges before the accused, brother. We must do this formally and in a dignified matter. Please, contain yourself.'

He gave a small cough and began, in a voice with a strange, chanting tone. Even his accent changed, as if he were trying to sound more English:

'These are the charges laid out against you, the varmint

known as Kai Breakwater. Do I take it your Christian name is Katherine?'

Kai nodded. So they knew. She was done for.

'Katherine Breakwater, you are charged with:

'Defiling God's House.

'Deceiving the brothers of our most noble cathedral, the Holy Trinity, also known as Christ Church.

'Inflicting the plague on the people of Dublin.

'Conversing with demons.

'Possession of a familiar, to wit, the black cat known as Dinny.

'Foully perverting the minds of the holy brothers in the election of Prior Stephen of Derby as prior to the said house of the Holy Trinity.

'What say you to these charges?'

Kai swallowed.

'I am not guilty of any of them. Except perhaps misleading the brothers into thinking I was a boy. But no one ever asked me if I was a girl!'

Brother Malcolm broke in: 'You see how devious she is, twisting the truth. Another charge against her, dissimulation to her judges! Shall we add it to the list?'

'Let's!' said Roland gleefully.

Brother Malcolm was writing everything down. Kai wondered should she just say nothing. Already it seemed that anything she might say could become yet another charge against her. But she had to defend herself, so she continued, 'And I don't believe that my singing has defiled God's house. I believe that God and his angels love to hear music, whether it comes from the mouth of a boy or a girl. As for the other charges – they are just ridiculous. I don't know how anyone could believe them. I certainly did not bring the plague or have anything to do with the election of Stephen as prior. Though I'm very glad he *was* elected. So there.'

Here she looked rebelliously at Brother Malcolm.

'Ah! See! She does not deny that she has a familiar. Or that she speaks to demons.' Brother Malcolm was smiling almost as widely as Roland.

'Dinny is a cat. A CAT.' Kai spelt it out. 'She is no more magic than I am. As for the voices in the cathedral, perhaps they are magic, but if they are, they are good magic. They are the voices of the children who have sung there through the years. They do no harm, and they comfort me. Jack is there too, and he is happy.'

She looked at Roland as she said this, hoping he at least would understand the importance of Jack still being with them in the cathedral, but he just looked away.

His father said, 'Blasphemy and sorcery! It is worse than I thought! We cannot let the people listen to her speak, she is too skilful with her lies. We should have guessed with her mountebank father that she would have a tongue like a serpent ...'

'You must realise that we have other witnesses against you. The mason Paul has also borne witness that he has heard the voices of demons in Christ Church. Confess and repent, child.' Brother Malcolm's voice had changed, become gentle: 'If you confess and repent there is the chance of a less painful death than burning. It is quite clear that you have magical powers. You have admitted it yourself with your talk of the spirits in the cathedral. And look how you walked among the plague victims and did not become ill. Look how you saved your friend the miller's boy.'

'Brother Albert and Dame Maria went into all the plague houses too, much more often than me. And no one is accusing them of witchcraft! And if I had been able to save lives, wouldn't I have saved Jack too?'

To her fury, Kai found that she was crying. The escheator said sternly.

'Enough of this. It is evident that the witch is guilty. She is a most stubborn sorceress. Let us spread the word in Dublin that she is to be punished!'

'But I have not been tried! There has been no court! You have made up your mind already so no matter what I say you are not going to believe me!'

'We will bring you before the people. We have spread the word and they will gather in the marketplace at first light, to be told of your crimes. They will judge.'

Kai had been too angry with the lies that were being told

about her to have been really afraid up until now. But now she realised that she was in very serious trouble. She had been judged by crowds before. Being part of a crowd sometimes brought out the worst in people, made them become cruel in a way they would never be normally. Nice people, gentle people, had been part of the crowds that had run her father and herself and Edward out of towns, pelting them with stones and shouting at them. Bring a crowd together and you could never tell what might happen, only that they were usually looking for someone to blame for all their problems. And in a town like Dublin, where the plague was present, they would be only too happy to have someone to blame ...

Her three judges left. She sat for what seemed like a long time, bound to the chair. Finally, a faint light appeared and Dame Rachel came down the steps to the cellar. She was dressed in a white shift and carried a bowl of soup and some bread. She untied Kai's hands, but not her legs, and handed her the food.

'Eat quickly,' she said. 'I should not be here.'

The soup was thin and greasy and the bread hard, but Kai was so grateful for something to eat that she ate everything. Dame Rachel tied her hands again, this time in front of her. She placed a small crucifix between her fingers. Then she noticed the coral on the ground.

'What's this?' she asked, picking it up.

Kai felt tears coming on.

'It was my mother's,' she said in a choked voice.

Dame Rachel slipped the coral into her tied hands and covered them with her own.

'You may be a witch and be going to burn,' she said. 'But that does not mean you may not have the comfort of the Lord and of your own mother with you. It may help you when the flames come to meet you.'

There I was thinking her as mad as a brush, thought Kai, and she's possibly saner and certainly kinder than her husband and son.

All the night through she sat, tied to the chair, with only the company of a small furry animal, who crept from the shadows into her lap and licked her hands with her tiny, rough tongue, trying to comfort her mistress, and, in the darkness, doing her very best to keep the rats away from her.

As soon as he could escape from Brother Albert, Tom headed for the cathedral. He was already feeling bad about having told Roland where Kai went when she sneaked away from them. When he saw that there was nobody in the cathedral, he felt worse. He spent the next half hour checking all the places in the priory where Kai was usually to be found. Then he left to see if his friend might have gone to Giles the mason's house. On his way there, he almost tripped over an urchin, who barrelled into him in too much of a hurry to watch where he was going. He gave Tom a cheeky grin.

'What's your hurry? You nearly tripped me up!' Tom said.

'I'm going to collect wood for the witch burning! The girl from the priory is going to be burned!' The child could hardly speak with excitement.

'What do you mean?' said Tom. 'There are no girls in the priory!'

'Yes there are! It's the choirboy called Kai, that everyone thought was a boy. Except she's a girl. And she's a witch so they are going to take her out at dawn to be burned! She ... she ...' the child thought hard, trying to remember exactly what he had been told and ended triumphantly: 'She converses with demons in the cathedral! Paul the mason heard them!'

Tom swallowed. What was going on? Demons in the cathedral? Had their trick been too successful? He was still trying to take in the fact that Kai was a girl. So that was why she was so secretive.

'Where is Kai?' he asked. 'Who has arrested him ... her?'

'Oh, nobody knows. But she is being brought to trial at the High Cross in the marketplace in the morning, at first light. They say that when she is burned the curse will be lifted from Dublin and the plague will end!'

Tom took a halfpenny out of his pocket. 'Run to the priory and tell Brother Albert all about this, and you shall have this. Will you do that? Do you promise me?'

The child nodded and took the coin. Then he ran off into the maze of streets. Tom could only hope he would keep his word.

Tom wondered what to do. If Kai was being guarded by the law, there was no point trying to find her. Perhaps if he went to the mason's house there might be some word as to where Edward was. It was a faint chance, but he didn't have a lot of choices.

At the mason's house, the door to the courtyard was locked and there was no answer when he banged on it as hard and as long as he could.

He was standing there, unsure what to do next, when a woman in a bright red gown, passing him in the street, stopped and stared hard at him. She was carrying a large wicker basket full of linens. He recognised her as Ymna, for she often did the washing for the priory.

She looked at him quizzically. 'No point trying that door, they are all gone away up to talk to the guild.'

'Is Joan with them? It's really her I'm looking for,' said Tom.

'She is. They have all gone up to get young Paul dismissed. It turns out he was the one who took that statue that there was all the fuss about. He wanted to get Edward into trouble. He finally confessed what he had done. Something must have put the frighteners on him; he keeps babbling about demon voices in the cathedral. Why did you want to see Joan?'

'I wanted to see if she had had any news from Edward. His sister is in terrible danger and needs help.'

Quickly, Tom told Ymna what had had happened to Kai. He ended: 'But I don't know where she is or who has captured her. And I don't know what to do!'

'I'll tell you what you can do, for I know Kai and Edward well, and their father. You must go and fetch Ned Breakwater from where he is up in the mountains. He is the only one with the wit to save his daughter.'

'But how? And where is he? How can I get up there?'

'I was heading up to the priory myself to tell Kai that I have finally got news of where Ned is. He's up in the hills beyond the village of Rathfarnham. It's a good two hours ride from the city. You must go out Patrick's Gate and follow the trail out towards Rathfarnham. After the church there, you will be going up into the hills. It will be a rough ride, for those mountains are full of danger. Ned is with the fairground people, so if you head south and ask for directions for their camp you will find the way. But you must go at once, before the dark sets in.'

'Is there no one else who can go?' said Tom, desperately.

Ymna snorted disdainfully.

'Yes, I'll head up there in my chariot and horses! No, boy, of course there is no one else. You are wasting time, go on now, get you gone. Do you want to see your friend burned alive?'

Tom drew in a deep breath. Who else could help? Joan? Brother Albert? It was true, he was the only one left to do this. He was going to have to take a horse from the priory stables and make his way through darkness up into the hills where the wild Irish lived. If only Jack were around to come with him!

Tom sat down on a bale of hay and eyed the priory horses nervously. There were three of them: Abelard, Anselma and the newest horse, Puca. Tom watched in frustration at the performance that Puca always put on when someone came near him. The horse danced its way around its stable, its eyes rolling, its mouth frothing.

Brother Albert, when he had been brought out to see the new horse, had looked at the fierce eyes and kicking coal black feet and had not been able to find a suitable saint or theologian to name him after.

In the end, Jack had chosen the horse's name, calling him after the fairy beast who brought travellers on wild midnight rides. Puca was the fastest horse in the stables. He was also the meanest. But Anselma was due to foal and Abelard was as lazy as sin, so Tom really didn't have much choice.

He gritted his teeth and stood up, halter in hand. He could not waste any more precious time, but it was going to be a nightmare, trying to catch the huge black beast without being kicked to pieces. He threw the halter in the general direction of Puca's neck but only managed to hit him on the side with it.

Puca went even more wild. 'Jack should be the one who is here doing this,' Tom thought bitterly. 'Jack should have been the one left alive. He would have been able to help Kai. Or whatever she is called.' He kicked the manger and cursed. The he started over again. After several more futile attempts to catch the horse, he finally made it onto Puca's back with all his bones more or less intact. Once on the horse, he made straight for the southern gate of the city.

Leaving Dublin to take the unfamiliar road was strange and frightening. The mountains rose up before him, blue darkening to purple as the light faded. He rode the horse as fast as he dared, trying hard not to imagine who – or what – could be lurking behind the hedgerows that lined the track to the hills. It was almost dark when he reached Rathfarnham. The village was nothing more than a scatter of cabins huddled around a small church. There was a woman standing outside one, gathering a basket of turf, and he stopped to ask the way to the fairground people's camp.

The farmer's wife looked at him curiously. 'And what might a city choirboy want with that gang of rascals? And riding such a fine horse?' she asked.

'Please, just tell me the way; it's urgent.' Not for the first time Tom wished he had Jack's easy manner. And his ability to make up stories at will, which would help him give an explanation which this woman would accept.

'Urgent, is it? Hmmh. Very well, then – take the trail that leads up past Harold's Grange, keeping the mountain in view all the time. Then you will have to ford the river – there's no bridge. The trail will finish and after that you will have to make your way through the scrub woodland and heather as best you can. The fairground people are camping in Kelly's Glen, to the west of the hilltop. You'll see their fires as you come near to them. But don't say I didn't warn you of how dangerous it is up there! There are dark creatures living in those woods. The Irish O'Tooles have taken over the Royal Deer Forest at Glencree, just the other side of the mountains. So these hills are no longer safe; it's not safe even down here in the village. And never mind the Irish, there are wicked creatures up there that are not human at all ...

'Didn't you ever hear stories of the black cat seen up there and the witches meeting the devil on those mountains?'

Thanks, thought Tom. That was all I needed, more horrors to be afraid of along the way. Every nerve in his body was taut and every bone in his body ached from the ride. Puca was restive, giving every indication of wanting to bolt back to his stable.

Not happening, you horrible beast, said Tom to himself. Holding tight onto the reins with his blistered hands, he directed the horse towards the louring darkness of the hills.

A bitter wind had sprung up and wailed through the trees that blocked his path southwards. There was still a long, hard ride ahead, and he wished he could believe that he would ever reach his goal.

The Singing Stones

It was dawn, and in the streets of Dublin there was pandemonium. The Watch had been called to try to control the crowd. Word had gone out about the witch, and people had gathered from all over the city to see the burning. It was said that this powerful enchantress was the cause of all the troubles of the city. Now she had been found and was going to be punished, perhaps the nightmare of plague would end.

Every urchin in Dublin was already happily collecting loose wood to build the bonfire, cursing because so much of it had already been used for the Halloween fires.

Crowds had gathered around the market cross. Dragged out from the escheator's house, there was a sudden silence when the crowd realised that the witch was a little girl. Many had expected to see a powerful enchantress. Instead, Kai stood in front of them, small and frail and pale as a ghost.

The escheator took the platform that had been hastily erected beside the bonfire site. Kai was dragged up beside him

and somebody threw Dinny onto the platform where she mewed and rubbed against Kai's legs. Kai wished she could pick her up to comfort her, but her hands were still tied together.

Silence fell as the crowd looked at the little girl and the cat. Many of the people there knew her as the choirboy who had visited their houses with Brother Albert. A whisper of surprise went around the gathering.

'Do not let her innocent appearance deceive you!' shouted Brother Malcolm, taking a place on the platform. 'For this exterior hides one of the most evil souls that I have ever come across in my life. Truly the Evil One can take many forms! This is the witch and blasphemer who has brought disaster on the town of Dublin! If we slay her, her powers will be destroyed and we will be free of this terrible contagion!'

Someone called up from the back of the crowd.

'How do you know she brought the plague?'

'Did not the contagion arrive at same time as she took up residence in the holy priory with the brothers? See, she has blasphemed by pretending to be a boy and thus gained access to the most sacred places of the church! She has spread her filth even among the good canons! Did she not kill her companion with her potions and her spells? Remember young Jack, the orphan boy; it was she who was responsible for his death!'

At this, Kai could keep silent no longer. She cried out: 'It's lies, it's all lies. I would have done anything to save Jack!'

But her voice was drowned out in the roars of the crowd. Someone began to chant: 'Burn the witch child! Burn the witch!' And numerous other voices joined in, so that it seemed to Kai as if a wave of hatred was washing around at her feet. When she looked down into the crowd, she could see nothing but malice and condemnation on the faces of everyone there. Even the children, some of them younger than her, were shouting as loudly as their parents. Some of them looked so small they could hardly have understood what they were saying, but that did not stop them shouting. A rotten egg suddenly hit her in the face and ran down her cheek. The smell was horrible, but she could do nothing to wipe it away.

'They really are going to kill me,' she thought. She desperately, wanted her father to come. He had got the family out of so many seemingly hopeless situations. She looked out over the crowd, as if she might see him in the distance, striding across with his long legs, joking, turning the mood of the crowd from hatred to laughter. But no one came – not even Tom or Brother Albert, or Edward or Dame Maria, any of those who might have spoken for her and tried to save her. And the sky darkened and the roar of the crowd grew louder and louder in the gloom of the November dawn. To the east the sky was red and orange, and the flames that had caught in the bonfire reflected the lurid colours and threw deeper shadows against the walls of the city.

And suddenly there was an outcry from the cathedral, and Brother Albert came rushing out.

'What are you doing?' he shouted above the crowd. 'What are you doing to that child?'

'She is a witch!' shouted Brother Malcolm. 'Do not try to defend her! You thought her a boy and she is a girl, who has deceived us and defiled the holy places! She must die!'

Brother Albert's face was very red, and he seemed to be almost in tears. He had spent the night trying to find out what had happened to Kai and Tom. An unknown child had run up to him in the street and tugged at his habit, whispering that Kai was in danger. He had a strong suspicion that the escheator and Roland were involved, but when he went to the Fitzhugh house on Skinner's Row he had not been allowed in. Prior Stephen had tried to talk to both Archbishop Bicknor and the Mayor of Dublin, Kenewrek Scherman, but both were ill, it was said with the plague. The canons had stayed up all night, praying, and Brother Albert called frantically now into the crowd:

'Rubbish! The child is no witch, even if she is a girl! She has given me help with the sick and the dying and the poor; she has sung like an angel in the church! How can she be evil?'

Roland chimed in, 'I have heard her conversing with

demons! How can she explain that? Paul heard the demons too! And Tom saw her in the cathedral!'

'Where is Tom, anyway?' Brother Albert looked around anxiously.

Now Brother Malcolm spoke,'Never mind that! I tell you she speaks to the spirits of air and darkness! Unholy beings from hell!'

'Burn the witch!'

The cry was taken up again by the mob, and they surged forward as if they would drag Kai from the platform and pull her towards the flames which were now licking greedily around the wood of the bonfires. Dame Maria had appeared beside Brother Albert and was trying to calm the voices, but no one was listening to her.

To Kai, looking down, it was as if the crowd itself had become possessed by some kind of demon. The voices of reason were drowned under the terrible need to find someone to blame for all the dreadful things that had happened to Dublin.

But just as the crowd had caught hold of Kai's dress, another commotion started. Everyone turned to see what was causing it. A loud and carrying voice rang out. At the head of a group of jugglers and tricksters, of musicians and fortune tellers and the rag tag and bobtail of the roads of Ireland, rode Ned Breakwater, also known as Longshanks, mounted on a piebald pony too small for him and singing loudly. On either side of him rode him Edward and Tom. He stopped abruptly when he saw his daughter.

'Well now, Kai, and what trouble have you got yourself into?' he asked.

Kai found that she was laughing. That had always been her question to him.

'It appears that these people think I am a witch, Pa.' Kai said. She was pleased to realise that her voice sounded quite calm.

'A witch! Indeed. And you such a law-abiding and virtuous young lady, I have sometimes wondered how you could be a child of mine. Good people, what proof have you that she is a witch?'

'She came at the same time as the plague!'

'She sings with demons and converses with them!'

'She has a black cat!'

'Indeed. A black cat. And are there no other black cats in Dublin? If there are, perhaps we should seek their owners out and burn them too. I think one such is owned by the mayor, and another by the Lady Rachel and her husband, the good escheator. As for coming to Dublin at the same time as the plague, why, is she not one of many such? One might as well blame the sheep farmers who came here selling their beasts at the end of summer fair. And if she is the cause of the plague, how is it that it has broken out in other towns? She was not in Kilkenny when the pestilence broke out there. As to the singing with demons, daughter, can you explain what all that is about?'

Kai took a breath. This was hard to explain, even to her father. But now her secret had to come out. She spoke slowly, choosing her words carefully.

'Father, after my friend Jack died, I went to the cathedral. And I sang for him. I felt very lonely and I just wanted to feel closer to him. And then something very strange happened. Something so strange, I can't explain it. I found there was a kind of echo in the walls. There was singing, voices that seemed to be coming from them. And then I found that it was Jack singing back, singing with me. And other voices joined in, the voices of the children who sung in the cathedral, right from the time it was first built. So I go there for comfort, and sometimes the voices tell me stories of the cathedral in times gone by. Surely, there is nothing wrong with this, even if it is magic? It does no harm to anyone, and it comforts me greatly.'

The escheator had broken in, 'We are wasting time here. What is this rabble that they should interrupt our judgements? Men of the Watch, arrest them and take them away, for the fairground people have been forbidden to enter the city.'

Ned laughed.

'That is true. But with all the Watch watching nought but this circus, t'was easy for us to come in. And I owe great thanks to this young lad for coming to fetch me.'

He smiled at Tom, who blushed fierily.

Kai suddenly felt fearful. What if the mob suddenly turned on her father and his friends? Had they been led into danger themselves? Were they risking their own lives to come and help her?

But now Ned Breakwater laughed again.

He gave a sign to his friends and suddenly the group surged forward to the platform. Kai found herself being lifted into her father's arms and placed before him on the piebald horse he was riding.

'Come, my friends. There is one way to find out the truth of this matter. Let us go to the cathedral and see if what the lass says is true. Let us hear these voices and see if they are good or evil. Then you may make your judgement on my child.'

Despite protests from the escheator and Brother Malcolm, there was a murmur of agreement from the crowd. Many of them, now they had had time to think, had begun to wonder if this small girl could really be the cause of all the troubles that had come upon the city of Dublin.

So Kai was carried from the High Cross to the great western door of the cathedral, and the crowd surged in after her. At the High Altar Kai was set down and the crowd, quiet now they were inside the church, looked on expectantly.

'Sing, daughter,' said Ned. 'Sing your heart out. Sing and

let us hear the voices.'

So Kai sang, and as she sang, she heard the voices joining in. First she heard Tom and Edward and her own father, then Dame Maria and Brother Albert and all the brothers but Brother Malcolm, then Ymna and Joan and Master Giles and his wife. But then the other voices joined in, the warm, bright voices of the children: Jack and Finn and all those who had sung in the cathedral since its foundation. And the music was so beautiful that every person there wondered how they could ever have been angry. And after the singing had finished, Brother Albert and Prior Stephen came forward. Prior Stephen said, 'How can you believe that such wonderful music, sung in praise of the Lord in his own house, can be evil? How could you think that? It is those who would have you harm this innocent child that are the evil ones. But let us leave it to God to punish them for their ill will towards her. Now let us all sing, and pray for forgiveness to the Lord and to Our Lady, that we may be freed from the will to harm that lives in our hearts.'

And so within the ancient walls of the cathedral the people of Dublin sang, sang in praise of creation and in thanks for the glory of the world, sang for comfort and courage and hope. And when they came outside, it was a bright and sunny day and the bells were ringing out from every church in the city.

The Blackbird in the Garden, April 1349

There was a blackbird singing in the garden of Dame Maria's house. A sign that spring was really here, thought Kai. This spring was bringing hope with it, because the plague was gradually loosening its grip on Dublin. The dark shadow that had lain over the city was finally lifting.

Soon her father would be here too, for he had promised to come to Dublin at Easter. Kai was doing some needlework, seated on a stone bench at the gate to the river, but she kept getting distracted. She was finding it difficult to keep the stitches straight, for the blackbird's song and the tolling of the Christ Church bell for vespers made it hard to keep her mind on her work. Being a girl was not all fun. Learning to wear skirts again had been hard at first, but she had got used to it. And how she loved her new blue dress. She stroked it thoughtfully, delighting in the feeling of the soft wool under her fingers.

Tom and the three new choirboys would be singing in the cathedral now. It would be the hymn in praise of the Queen of Heaven, the *Salve Regina*. She hummed the music quietly to herself. Sometimes she missed the choir badly. She had loved to hear her voice joining with the others; she had loved the way they blended together to make something beautiful. That was one of the things she had learned from the choir. Voices singing together could make a kind of beauty that one voice singing alone could never make. Of course, she sang at Mass with all the other people and alone with Tom sometimes, but it was not the same as when the four of them – yes, even Roland had had his part to play – had been together in the choir. Sometimes she missed other parts of her old life too. She even missed the lessons with Brother Albert, although Dame Maria was helping her to keep up her Latin and her reading. She had come to stay in Dame Maria's house, and now she loved her even more than she had when she had seemed a distant and angelic figure. She had learned that Dame Maria could be as testy as Brother Albert when things were not done to her satisfaction, and that needlework could be as boring to learn as any other task. But she was happy. She could see Tom when she liked and she visited the canons often. Edward had come back to Dublin where he was making great advances with his craft.

Her father had stayed in the city until after Christmas, but then he had taken off out onto the roads again.

'Dame Maria would give you work, if you wished,' Kai had said to him. 'She said there is always work for a man of your wit and strength.'

'You can't keep an old dog tied up for too long,' he had said to her. 'I need the open road and the chance of adventure.'

But he had promised to come back to visit regularly. Sometimes Kai made up stories to herself about her father and Dame Maria getting married, but she knew they were only stories. She could not imagine him staying in Dame Maria's quiet and orderly house. It would very soon stop being quiet and orderly.

Kai smiled to herself and leaned back against the apple tree. Primroses and the first forget-me-nots grew at her feet and budding apple-blossom surrounded her. Dinny slept in a ray of sunlight on the bench beside her. The water of the Liffey lapped against the walls of the garden and Kai thought of Jack. She still missed him, though no longer with the same grief she had felt in the early days. His spirit, she knew, lived on, in her memory and in the music and even in the very stones of the cathedral. Tom had been given his wish and was to return to the mill after Easter, to take up his father's trade. His voice had started to break and he had finally plucked up the courage to tell Brother Albert that he had no desire to become a monk. Brother Albert had been not been surprised, though he had been sad.

'I have lost every one of my best choristers,' he had said forlornly. For now even Roland had left the priory. The escheator, after his humiliating defeat in front of the people of Dublin, had left for England and taken Roland with him, leaving Dame Rachel to her fanaticisms. Brother Malcolm too had left. No one knew where he had gone. He had simply disappeared one night, with coins from the collection plate and a side of lamb that the kitchener had been saving for the Easter celebrations.

Kai was content. She knew she would be here to see the apple and pear blossom ripen into fruit. She was safe and settled in this garden in this city.

The city holds us all, she thought. All of us who are here now and all of us who have ever been here. All of us who will be here in time to come. It holds the cathedral too, safe inside its walls. And the cathedral holds all the voices of the children. She smiled suddenly, thinking of something else. I'm only a very tiny part of it all, she thought. Yet I myself hold all of it inside me, because I am sitting here, thinking about it.

Now as the light faded, the blackbird's song grew louder, climbing high, stronger than the fading notes of the bell. He sang out his final note and there was suddenly quiet in the garden. In the light-filled moment between the clear notes of the blackbird and dying call of the bell, something, neither silence nor song, echoed back from the cathedral stones, where, like a great bird resting from its flight, it brooded quietly over the city below.

HISTORICAL NOTES

WHEN WAS CHRIST CHURCH FOUNDED?

The cathedral of the Holy Trinity, better known as Christ Church, was founded *c*1030, by Dúnán, first bishop of Dublin. The land it stands on was granted to him by Sitric 'Silkbeard', the Viking king of the city.

The cathedral came under Anglo-Norman control after their arrival in the 1170s, and was rebuilt shortly afterwards under Archbishop John Cumin.

ST LAURENCE O'TOOLE

This is also the period when St Laurence O'Toole (whose reputed heart relic is still held in the cathedral) introduced the rule of St Augustine to the cathedral, and the cathedral would remain staffed by these Augustinian canons until the Reformation. St Laurence was also known as a peacemaker during the upheaval of the Anglo-Norman period, and is believed to have saved the lives of many orphans and other Dubliners through his negotiating skills.

FROM THE CHRIST CHURCH RECORDS

The records of Christ Church detail disasters such as the fire of 1283 and the storm which damaged the belfry in 1316. The cathedral and the adjoining priory played a very important role in the political and social life of Dublin.

PRIORY LIFE, HELL, THE DOLOCHER, GREENTEETH JENNY AND THE BLACK DEATH

An account roll of the cathedral priory covering the period 1337–1346 is the source of much of the detail in *Where the Stones Sing,* including the name of the washerwoman, Ymna. The detail of priory life and the layout of the buildings as recounted in the book is accurate, with the exception of the description of Hell, which is only mentioned in later accounts. The Dolocher and Greenteeth Jenny are also later creations of folk imagination. The Christ Church clergy were known as 'canons' at the time of the story, but they are addressed in the novel as 'brothers', which was the usual term used for monks during the medieval period.

The Black Death, however, was a very real part of the history of Dublin, first appearing in late summer 1348 and continuing to ravage the city well into 1349. The annalist John Clyn records that 14,000 people died in Dublin of the plague between the beginning of August and Christmas in 1348. One reason for the devastation caused by the plague was lack of medical knowledge. No connection was made between the presence of fleas from black rats and the spread of the disease. The mayor of Dublin Kenewrek Scherman and Archbishop Bicknor of Dublin were both said to have died of the plague. It is possible that Prior Robert [de Hereforde] was also a victim of the epidemic.

MUSIC AND THE CATHEDRAL

Stephen de Derby became prior of Christ Church between 1347–49 and was responsible for the creation of the Christ Church psalter, a wonderfully illustrated manuscript showing the musical arrangement for the psalms sung by the canons in the cathedral. Music was an important part of the liturgy, although Christ Church did not have a choir school before the fifteenth century. In the interests of the story, Brother Albert's school has been moved to the time of the Black Death. In 1480, the cathedral was given a grant for four choristers by the family of the mayor of Dublin. The choir school was founded in 1493. Music has continued to be a hugely important part of the cathedral ceremonies, with the tradition of singing and bell-ringing continuing right up until the present day.

POLITICAL LIFE

Politically, the cathedral was an important centre of activity. In 1487, Lambert Simnel was crowned as King Edward VI, in an unsuccessful attempt by the Yorkists to wrest the throne of England from Henry VII. Politics intervened again at the time of the Reformation, when the relics of the cathedral, such as the Staff of Jesus and the Speaking Cross were publicly burned and the priory was dissolved. From this point on the cathedral was under the control of a Dean and Chapter, and no longer connected with the Augustinian order.

Despite the disaster of 1562, when the south wall of the nave of the cathedral collapsed bringing the roof with it, the church remained an important part of the civic life of Dublin. During the seventeenth century the law courts occupied the old monastic buildings adjoining the cathedral. As the years passed, the cathedral buildings suffered more and more from the ravages of time. But it was not until towards the end of the nineteenth century that George Edmund Street undertook the restoration and rebuilding of the cathedral, an enormous project funded by Henry Roe. After its completion Christ Church took its present appearance. The cathedral continues today as a centre for worship and a significant part of the heritage of the city. Its bells and its music still call out to the people of Dublin.

FOLLOW IN KATE'S FOOTSTEPS

If you visit the cathedral, you will be able to see some of the parts described in this story: the pillar with the musicians carved on it, the pilgrim foxes, the child's tomb. You will also see the mummified body of the cat chasing the rat, which I took as my inspiration for the important part cats play in the story.

Eithne Massey

THE STORIES BEHIND THE PHOTOGRAPHS

Prologue: Christ Church cathedral viewed from the east.

Chapter 1: A woman's head on a pillar on the north side of the nave, dating from around the 1230–40s. Wearing a crown, she was probably a noblewoman, and perhaps even a patron of the cathedral.

Chapter 2: The medieval brass lectern made *c*1500 most likely in England.

Chapter 3: A tile showing two birds facing each other.

Chapter 4: Lion heads in the tiled floor in the south ambulatory and the south aisle of the nave.

Chapter 5: This man's face was carved in the 1870s. He may be a stroke victim or a mason who was injured working on the cathedral. He can be found on the third pillar from the west on the south side of the nave.

Chapter 6: The cathedral's medieval book of obits mentions the 'brothers of the congregation'. This carving in a chair behind the high altar is said to represent the brotherhood of the cathedral and was adopted by the Friends of the cathedral. It is made up of three crowns with three fleur de lis surrounding a rose.

Chapter 7: A head corbel of a man with a fringe and side curls supporting a springer in the southwest corner of the west bay of the north aisle.

Chapter 8: A woman's head, carved in the 1870s, is on the fourth pillar from the west on the south side of nave. Her costume includes a barbette (band under chin) and coif (or pill-box) and is a typical idealised Victorian view of the medieval.

Chapter 9: A mural tablet displaying a shield of the Usher family. It may have been from a house in Fishamble Street which bore the arms of Sir Christopher Ussher, a serjeant-at-arms active in the late 16th century. It was probably taken into the cathedral when the house was demolished, along with many others in the area, by the Wide Streets Commissioners in the early 19th century.

Chapter 10: A mid-thirteenth-century cowled figure, perhaps a grimacing imp on the fourth pillar from the west on the north side of the nave.

Chapter 11: A mid-thirteenth-century monkey-head stop over the third pillar from the west on the north side of the nave.

Chapter 12: A tomb slab, *c*1300, possibly for a wealthy layman. The curls are a little unclerical for a monk. It may have been found in the ruins of the chapter house during the excavations in 1886.

Chapter 13: This startled man (perhaps a jester from the head dress) is a headstop on the east side of the first pillar on the northside of the nave.

Epilogue: Victorian reproductions of medieval tiles found during the restoration of the cathedral in the 1870s.

Information courtesy of Dr Stuart Kinsella, Research Advisor,
Christ Church Cathedral, Dublin